PHASE_

ΛDVΛNTΛGE

The Future of Immersive Cybersecurity Education

CERTIFIED

Disaster Response & Recovery Manager

EXAM PREP GUIDE

Michael I. Kaplan	Robert M. Peterson
(Author)	(Editor)

01

C)DRRM Certification Exam Vouchers

Vouchers to purchase the C)DRRM certification exam can be secured via the Phase2 Advantage office. Please see the last page of this exam prep guide for additional information and a **10% discount** off the exam fee when taken separately from a class.

Certified Disaster Response and Recovery Manager
C)DRRM Exam Prep Guide
Copyright © 2021 by Phase2 Advantage

Phase2 Advantage
P.O. Box 14071
Savannah, GA 31416
(912) 335-2217

Phase2 Advantage textbooks and study guides may be purchased at discounted rates for educational, business, or governmental use when bulk orders are required. For information, please contact our office at info@phase2advantage.com.

ISBN-13: 978-1734064001

COURSE DESCRIPTION

Business Continuity and Disaster Response and Recovery is the development of processes, policies, and procedures that prepare for and react to significant and unplanned operational disruptions. The *Certified Disaster Response and Recovery Manager* training course prepares students for industry certification in Business Continuity Planning and Disaster Recovery missions.

Facing daily risks to long-term success from a wide range of threats—cyber-attacks, human error, technical failures, and natural disasters—businesses must create practical plans to sustain their vital operations, security posture, industry reputation, and brand. Students will cover critical topics such as BCP Design and Development Strategies, Selection of Risk Management Frameworks, Qualitative and Quantitative Analysis Strategies, Creating Asset Inventories and Resource Profiles, Recovery Site Management and Workflows, Reviewing Cloud Computing Service Agreements, Cloud Data Security Strategies, and the Impact of Legal Requirements on Cloud Storage Solutions.

SUGGESTED READING

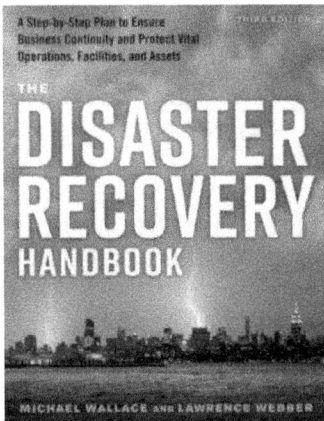

With the detailed guidance found in the thoroughly updated The Disaster Recovery Handbook, your company's survival and the speedy resumption of business is all but assured. Learn how to proactively assess risk, create recovery procedures, safeguard vital records, and more! And when the unavoidable, unpredictable disasters occur, you will know that you have planned for every contingency and have ensured that your company is responsible, ready, and resilient.

Paperback: 544 Pages
Publisher: AMACOM; Third edition (December 28, 2017)
ISBN-10: 0814438768
ISBN-13: 978-0814438763

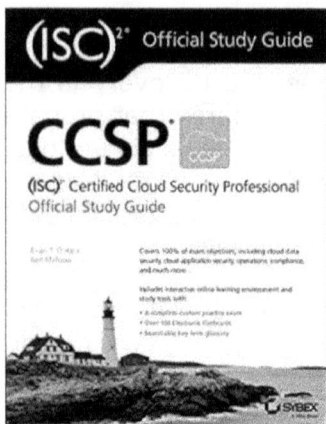

(ISC)² Official Study Guide

CCSP

(ISC)² Certified Cloud Security Professional Official Study Guide

The only official study guide for the new CCSP exam. CCSP (ISC)2 Certified Cloud Security Professional Official Study Guide is your ultimate resource for the CCSP exam. Covering all CCSP domains, this book walks you through cloud platform and infrastructure security, architectural concepts and design requirements, cloud data security, cloud application security, operations, and legal and compliance with real-world scenarios to help apply your skills along the way.

Paperback: 384 Pages
Publisher: Sybex; 1 edition (May 15, 2017)
ISBN-10: 1119277418
ISBN-13: 978-1119277415

ABOUT THE DIRECTOR

Michael I. Kaplan is the Director of Operations for Phase2 Advantage, a cybersecurity training and publishing company based in Savannah, Georgia. He is the Chairman of the Savannah Technical College Cybersecurity Advisory Committee and heavily involved in curriculum design. Michael has written numerous courses and cybersecurity training programs for corporate, academic, and government personnel. He has also developed training programs for Law Enforcement and Fugitive Task Force Investigators on the topics of Criminal Topology, Forensic Document Analysis, and Investigations. Michael's technical areas of specialization are Incident Handling and Response, Network Forensics, Digital Forensics, and Information Technology Risk Management. He also provides consulting services for government, corporate, and academic organizations both domestically and internationally.

Table of Contents

Knowledge Assessment Answer Key 253

Certification Exam Voucher 319

[This page intentionally left blank.]

DOMAIN 01

Introduction to Disaster Response Management

What is "Disaster Recovery"?

While the definition of Disaster Recovery differs from entity to entity, the course content will be based on the following definition:

Disaster Recovery:

A set of policies, tools, and procedures to enable the recovery and continuation of mission-critical technology infrastructure and systems following a natural or human-induced disaster.

Business Continuity Planning (BCP) and Disaster Recovery Planning (DRP) are both a combination of three primary disciplines with three distinct missions supporting the highest probability of successful BCP/DRP outcomes. These are the three pillars of the "BCP/DRP Tower;" if one of the pillars is missing the tower will most likely fall.

1. Certification and Accreditation Compliance
2. Risk Management and Audit
3. Business Process Alignment

There are a number of key definitions associated with disciplines of BCP/DRP that will be used throughout this course. For the sake of clarity and to reduce confusion, these key definitions have been listed below.

Event:

Any user- or system-generated action or occurrence that can be identified by a program and has significance for system hardware or software.

Incident:

Any unlawful, unauthorized, or unacceptable action that involves a computer system, cell phone, tablet, and any other electronic device with an operating system, or that operates in a computer network.

Maximum Allowable Downtime (MAD):

The absolute maximum time that systems can be unavailable without serious and/or negative impact to the organization.

Recovery Time Objective (RTO):

The targeted duration of time within which a mission-critical business process must be restored after a disaster and/or disruption in order to avoid unacceptable consequences associated with a break in business continuity.

Recovery Point Objective (RPO):

The maximum acceptable amount of data loss, measured in time, that can be incurred without serious and/or negative impact to the organization.

Quantitative Analysis:

The process of collecting and evaluating measurable and verifiable data in order to understand the condition and performance of a business.

Qualitative Analysis:

Examination and evaluation of non-measurable data using subjective judgement and non-quantifiable methods.

Map BCP to Organizational Objectives

Information Security is **not** a business objective in and of itself, but Information Security underlies **all** business objectives. It is important that BCP Managers map their security needs to organizational objectives to get support from senior leadership. A few examples of these objectives are listed below.

1. Maintain Corporate Profit Margin
2. Legal and Regulatory Compliance
3. Maintain a Competitive Advantage
4. Increase and Protect Brand Value
5. Continued Delivery of Products and Services

Business Continuity Planning (BCP)

The BCP is not a monolithic or linear document. Supported from the top-down and created from the bottom-up, it is a collection of plans that are always evolving.". The BCP consists of five primary plans, although the number can vary between entities based on need and context. Each of these plans and their functions will be discussed in further detail later in this domain.

1. The Administrative BCP
2. The Technical BCP
3. The Work Area BCP
4. The Epidemic / Pandemic BCP
5. The Crisis Management Plan

Disaster Recovery Planning (DRP)

Like its BCP counterpart, the DRP is not a monolithic or linear document and has many moving parts that are executed simultaneously. Additionally, like its BCP counterpart, the DRP consists of five primary plans, although the number can vary between entities based on need and context. Each of these plans and their functions will be discussed in further detail later in this domain.

1. The Data Recovery Plan
2. The Incident Response Plan
3. The Vulnerability Assessment Plan
4. The Network Forensics Plan
5. The Digital Forensics Plan

Being equally vital, each plan will have a significant part to play in the BCP/DRP mission, and they are not presented here in an order of importance. Each will have a significant part to play in the BCP/DRP mission.

The Administrative Continuity Plan

This plan is a consolidated, high-level document written to meet a set of specific business needs, and in a manner that makes sense to the senior leadership. Each plan will change from entity to entity based on organizational needs and context. Listed below are a few common topics that are typically addressed in these high-level plans.

1. **How Company BCP will be Conducted**: This section will outline the overall BCP leadership, strategy, development, and implementation. It will define the scope of the BCP and serve as the written support for the plan by senior leadership.

2. **Long-Term Contingency Planning**: This section will outline long-term contingency strategies based on the vision for the organizational mission.

3. **Common Reference Information**: This section will contain high-level reference information such as organizational charts, list of key vendors, list of key customers, critical assets, and critical personnel as determined in the Business Impact Analysis (to be discussed in the next domain).

4. **Description of Testing Expectations**: This section will outline the scope and frequency of testing both the BCP and the DRP, the reporting of test results, and the metrics associated with stated goals and successful outcomes.

5. **Keeping Pace with Process Changes**: This section will outline the change management system, version control system, and internal processes that ensure the BCP and DRP remain both relevant and current.

The Technical Continuity Plan

This plan is a detailed document, managed by IT leadership, and written to meet a set of specific technical needs, and in a manner that makes sense to the senior leadership. Each plan will change from entity to entity based on organizational needs and context. Listed below are a few common considerations that are typically addressed in these plans.

1. **Not Restricted to IT**: This plan is compiled and managed by IT, but it is not restricted to IT staff. It must be accessible to anyone expected to be a part of the technical recovery effort.

2. **Addresses All Technical Processes**: Very few leaders are aware of all the behind-the-scenes technical processes that support the vital business functions they manage.

3. **Only Addresses Vital Business Functions**: Only technical process that support vital business functions should be addressed.

4. **Written by Interdisciplinary Technicians**: This plan is typically written by an interdisciplinary team representing all IT functions in an organization.

5. **Make Process Easy for Technicians**: There is no guarantee the primary technician of a process will be the one tasked with executing elements of this plan. It should be written in such a manner as to allow any competent technician to follow the plan.

The Work Area Continuity Plan

This plan is a detailed document, maintained and managed by BCP leadership, and written to meet a set of specific workflow needs. It focuses on establishing a temporary work area for staff during a recovery process. An IT recovery is useless without an environment that allows key personnel to function in their roles. If staff cannot function, the competition is operating while the organization is not. It also provides the secondary benefit of enhancing the reputation and brand image of the organization, as customers tend to have more faith in an organization that has planned to continue operating under the most adverse circumstances.

The Epidemic and Pandemic Continuity Plan

This plan is a detailed document written to meet a set of specific staffing needs during the life cycle of an epidemic or pandemic. It is different from other plans in that it addresses an issue that can be foreseen but has a life cycle longer than other disasters. This plan considers a number of issues applicable to pandemics and serious epidemics.

1. It Affects People at all Levels
2. It Affects Organizations at all Levels
3. It Affects Upstream and Downstream Dependencies

The Crisis Management Plan

This plan is a detailed document written to meet a set of specific response and mitigation needs during an adverse situation. Each plan will change from entity to entity based on organizational needs and context. Listed below are a few common considerations that are typically addressed in these plans.

1. Incident Identification and Reporting
2. Incident Escalation Procedures
3. Incident Handling Policies
4. Stakeholder Notification Procedures
5. Disaster Recovery Initiation Procedures

The Incident Response Plan

This plan is a detailed document written to identify and characterize serious events possessing the capability of negatively impacting business operations. It outlines how leads of value will be defined, how incident timelines will be created, and how investigative priorities will be determined. This plan guides incident handling personnel in discovering the scope of the incident, and documents policies and standards for the creation and maintenance of case notes. Each plan will change from entity to entity based on organizational needs and context. Listed below are the six common stages of incident response that are typically addressed in these plans.

1. Detection
2. Analysis
3. Containment
4. Eradication
5. Recovery
6. Lessons Learned

The Vulnerability Assessment Plan

This plan is a detailed document, usually managed by Information Security Management, that is written to discover hidden flaws and weaknesses within critical business systems. Each plan will change from entity to entity based on organizational needs and context. Listed below are five common areas of interest that are typically addressed in these plans.

1. Modeling Attack Chains and Life Cycles
2. Targeted Active Vulnerability Scanning
3. Securely Deploying Architectural Assets
4. Passive Remediation and Containment
5. Offensive Threat Intelligence

The Network Forensics Plan

This plan is a detailed document written to identify the scope and impact of serious network security incidents. A few examples of such incidents are security breaches, data exfiltration, and incidents caused by malicious insiders. Each plan will change from entity to entity based on organizational needs and context. Listed below are five common areas of interest that are typically addressed in these plans.

1. Establishing Live Response Policies
2. Selection of Live Response Tools and Practices
3. System and Data Duplication Priorities
4. Creating Investigative and Analysis Methodologies
5. The Collection and Preservation of Evidence

The Digital Forensics Plan

This plan is a detailed document written to meet a set of specific remediation needs during an adverse situation. A few examples of such situations include malware triage, violations of an acceptable use policy, and utilizing the organizational network for criminal activity. Each plan will change from entity to entity based on organizational needs and context. Listed below are six common areas of consideration that are typically addressed in these plans.

1. Defining Forensic Goals and Objectives
2. Use of In-House or Out-Sourced Expertise
3. Legal Considerations for Network Devices
4. Evidence Collection and Chain-of-Custody Policies
5. Malware Triage and Analysis
6. Notification of External Law Enforcement Agencies

Challenges to the Desired State of Security

The desired state of security is defined as the difference between the current state of security and the state of security that would best protect the goals of the organization. Ideally, the key stakeholders within the organization would share common goals and objective perspectives on the desired state of security. In reality, the desired state must be defined in business and security terms while facing many common obstacles, such as the challenges listed below.

1. **Overconfidence and Unrealistic Optimism**: This is by far the most common issue any BCP Manager must overcome. In the first instance, leadership believes the organization can handle any adverse circumstance with little or no planning. In the second instance, leadership thinks the organization will never experience the adverse circumstance in question. Both share equally bad outcomes.

2. **Psychological Anchoring**: This is a bias present in the decision-making process where one piece of information is given disproportional consideration and importance. This bias is maintained despite any new information that may challenge the assumption and causes a fixation that excludes consideration of other facts.

3. **Status Quo Bias**: This is another common issue for BCP Managers to overcome and presents itself in phrases such as, "*It's always been done this way; if it isn't broken, don't try to fix it.*"

4. **Mental Accounting**: Mental accounting refers to the various values people place on money, based on personal and subjective criteria, that often has detrimental results. An example would be someone who values a "personal fund" of cash in a piggy bank more valuable than cash spent on paying down credit card debt, even though reducing the debt ultimately yields a better financial position than hiding cash.

5. **Herd Instinct**: This behavior is demonstrated when individuals act collectively as a group, with no type of centralized leadership, often in a contrary fashion to their individual beliefs or knowledge. This is also referred to as a "mob mentality."

6. **False Consensus**: This behavior is demonstrated when an individual believes their thoughts to reflect those of others, even if no consensus actually exists. This is seen primarily in decision-makers.

Defining Authority Documents

Organizational authority, accountability, responsibility, and purpose are defined by authority documents. Although they are considered to formal and definitive, BCP Managers must recognize that organizational culture can create "shadow policies" that serve to diminish or even negate established formal, written authority documents. There are five general types of authority documents that guide organizational activity, but one must always be aware of the role culture plays in power dynamics.

1. Policies
2. Standards
3. Guidelines
4. Procedures
5. Frameworks

The Evolution of Sustainable Policies

Organizational policies are created via an iterative process that is constantly evolving. As BCP policies are created they will experience the same evolutionary process. The first draft of any policy is rarely adequate, and the maturity level of policies tend to be incremental by nature. Below are five common phases policies experience as they mature.

1. **Initial**:   Ad Hoc and/or no Formality
2. **Developing**: Informal and Basic Structure
3. **Defined**:   Organization-Wide but Lack Controls
4. **Managed**:   Defined Roles and Measured Results
5. **Optimized**: Culturally Entrenched and Practiced

Plan Activation Challenges

Challenges to BCP/DRP activation will be discussed in detail in the following domains, but it important for BCP Managers to design solutions that account for real-world challenges, not unrealistic solutions created to appease senior management.

DOMAIN 01

Introduction to Disaster Response Management

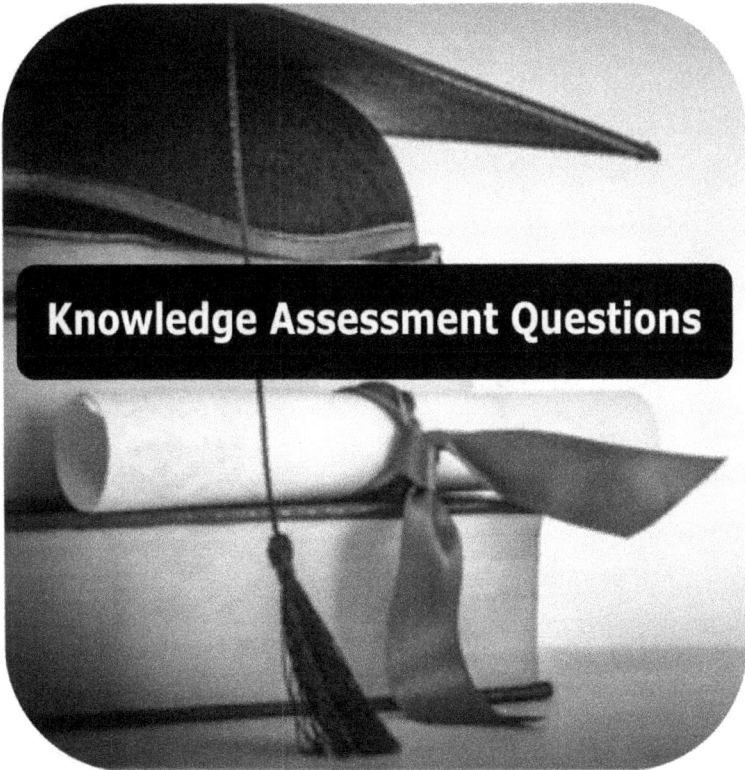

Knowledge Assessment Questions

The following knowledge assessment questions are presented as true / false, multiple choice, and fill-in-the-blank. The correct answers are provided in an Answer Key at the end of the text. These questions may or may not be presented on the actual certification exam.

Domain 01: Knowledge Assessment Questions

1. *"A set of policies, tools, and procedures to enable the recovery and continuation of mission-critical technology infrastructure and systems following a natural or human-induced disaster."*

A. Business Continuity

B. Incident Handling

C. Disaster Recovery

D. Business Impact Analysis

E. None of the Above

2. _____ is a set of policies, tools, and procedures to enable the recovery and continuation of mission-critical technology infrastructure and systems following a natural or human-made disaster.

A. Business Continuity

B. Incident Handling

C. Disaster Recovery

D. Information Security

E. None of the Above

3. *"Any user- or system-generated action or occurrence that can be identified by a program and has significance for system hardware or software."*

A. Event

B. Incident

C. Security Breach

D. Disaster

E. None of the Above

4. The three pillars of Business Continuity Planning (BCP) and Disaster Recovery Planning (DRP) are certification and compliance, risk management and audit, and _____.

A. Training and Awareness

B. Management Support

C. Effective Communication

D. Operational Process Alignment

E. None of the Above

5. *"The absolute maximum time that systems can be unavailable without serious and/or negative impact to the organization."*

A. Technical Maintenance Window (TMW)

B. Recovery Point Objective (RPO)

C. Maximum Allowable Downtime (MAD)

D. Recovery Time Objective (RTO)

E. None of the Above

6. A(n) _____ is a detailed document, maintained and managed by BCP leadership, written to meet a set of specific workflow needs.

A. Technical Continuity Plan

B. Work Area Continuity Plan

C. Administrative Continuity Plan

D. Crisis Management Plan

E. None of the Above

7. *"The maximum acceptable amount of data loss, measured in time, that can be incurred without serious and/or negative impact to the organization."*

A. Technical Maintenance Window (TMW)

B. Recovery Point Objective (RPO)

C. Maximum Allowable Downtime (MAD)

D. Recovery Time Objective (RTO)

E. None of the Above

8. A(n) _____ is a detailed document, maintained and managed by IT leadership, written to meet a set of specific technology needs.

A. Technical Continuity Plan

B. Work Area Continuity Plan

C. Administrative Continuity Plan

D. Crisis Management Plan

E. None of the Above

9. "*The examination and evaluation of non-measurable data using subjective judgement and non-quantifiable methods.*"

A. Financial Analysis

B. Qualitative Analysis

C. Predictive Analysis

D. Quantitative Analysis

E. None of the Above

10. A(n) _____ is a detailed document written to meet a set of specific response and mitigation needs during an adverse situation.

A. Technical Continuity Plan

B. Work Area Continuity Plan

C. Administrative Continuity Plan

D. Crisis Management Plan

E. None of the Above

11. Which choice below represents a challenge to the activation of a Business Continuity Plan (BCP)?

A. Initial News Reports can be Speculative

B. Level of Impact is Typically Unknown

C. Access to Site can be Restricted

D. Initial Information is Typically Minimal

E. All of the Above

12. A(n) _____ is a consolidated, high-level document written to meet a set of specific business and operational needs.

A. Technical Continuity Plan

B. Work Area Continuity Plan

C. Administrative Continuity Plan

D. Crisis Management Plan

E. None of the Above

13. Information Security is a critical business objective in and of itself, and Information Security drives all business objectives.

1. True

2. False

14. Corporate culture can create "shadow policies" that serve to diminish or even negate established formal, written policies.

1. True

2. False

15. The Digital Forensics Plan is a general document written to meet a set of specific planning needs when converting data to digital media.

1. True

2. False

16. The Incident Response Plan is a detailed document written to identify and characterize serious events possessing the capability of negatively impacting business operations.

1. True

2. False

17. The Business Continuity Plan (BCP) is a monolithic and linear document. It is supported bottom-up, created top-down, and changes every five years.

1. True

2. False

18. The first draft of a policy is rarely adequate, and the maturity level of policies tend to be incremental by nature.

1. True

2. False

Overview of The Business Impact Analysis

Roles of a Business Impact Analysis

1. **Role 01**: The BIA is an analysis of the important functions that are essential to the operation of the business.

2. **Role 02**: The BIA is used to quantify and qualify the value of each function to the business.

3. **Role 03**: The BIA is used to identify the risks posed to the most valuable business functions.

4. **Role 04**: The BIA is used to suggest mitigation actions to reduce the likelihood or impact of identified risks.

5. **Role 05**: The BIA is used to indicate how much is lost per hour or per day for the length of the outage.

6. **Role 06**: The BIA is used to identify the IT systems associated with critical business functions.

Benefits of a Business Impact Analysis

A BIA provides many benefits to the organization, many of which are valuable beyond the scope of a business continuity project. It may identify operational efficiencies or inefficiencies, assets not yet recorded, and provide better insight into the opportunities available for security to align with business processes. Benefits will change from entity to entity based on organizational needs and context. Listed below are seven direct benefits typically provided by a well-conducted BIA.

1. Identify Critical Functions to Protect
2. Identify Tangible Costs of Functions
3. Identify Intangible Costs of Functions
4. Identify Critical Resources for Functions
5. Determine Recovery Time Objectives
6. Identify Vital Business Records
7. Prioritize the Use of Scarce Resources

Domain 02: *Overview of The Business Impact Analysis*

BIA: Tangible Financial Costs

There are numerous ways the loss of a critical function can have a negative financial impact on the organization. Tangible costs are those which can be accurately measured, calculated, and recorded on a balance sheet. Tangible losses will vary from entity to entity, but they all have one common denominator: they are real financial losses and objective by nature. Listed below are five examples of tangible losses that may be experienced by an organization.

1. Products Cannot be Shipped
2. Services Cannot be Delivered
3. Increased Waste from Spoilage
4. Penalties Imposed by Customers (SLA Breaches)
5. Legal Penalties for Non-Compliance (Regulatory Issues)

BIA: Intangible Financial Costs

Intangible costs due to the loss of a vital business function can be more difficult to identify but are no less damaging. They may present themselves as delayed costs after the recovery has been successfully executed and vital business functions have been restored. Intangible costs will change from entity to entity based on organizational structures and context. Listed below are five examples of intangible costs an organization may experience.

1. Loss of Customer Goodwill
2. Reduced Confidence in the Marketplace
3. Higher Employee Turnover
4. Damage to the Image and/or Brand
5. Loss of Faith in Senior Management by Stakeholders

Managing a BIA Project

Managing a BIA project is not a simple task that can be assigned to any volunteer. Additionally, the project must be supported both financially and politically from the highest levels of leadership in the organization. Listed below are five high-level functions the BIA project must accomplish to be successful.

1. **Conducted as an Individual Project**: The BIA must be approached as a standalone project and not be added as an afterthought to other existing initiatives.

2. **Approve the Project Budget**: Those responsible for the project must possess the ability to secure financial backing from senior leadership to ensure the highest probability of a successful outcome.

3. **Convey the Importance of Participation**: The project is interdisciplinary by nature and will require participation of key managers and personnel with little time to spare and little interest in the project itself. The projects' importance must be conveyed in a manner that convinces everyone they have some type of benefit by participating.

4. **Address Objections and Questions**: Those responsible for the project will be required to answer questions about the projects' scope and purpose and overcome objections from those who are reluctant to reveal what they consider to be sensitive information.

5. **Approve the Report for Submission**: Once the project has been concluded the report must be reviewed, compiled, edited, and approved for submission to senior leadership.

Selecting a BIA Project Manager

A well-run BIA project will build credibility for the overall disaster recovery planning project; a poorly run BIA project will be a disaster of its own making. Selection of the proper project manager is one of the most important decisions in the entire BIA process. The person must possess a high level of integrity as every facet of the organization will be exposed in this process.

A significant level of knowledge regarding the organization is needed to understand and know the true value of internal functions and processes. The person must be comfortable moderating discussions between key organizational units, as conversations about a functions' criticality tend to become heated quickly.

BIA Data Collection (Part I)

An effective data collection process will help quantify the value of each function in terms of financial and legal impacts. This phase in the data collection process is formal, structured, and critical to the success of the BIA project. The collection process typically involves the use of questionnaires, interviews, and training seminars.

Collection methods will change from entity to entity based on organizational needs and context. Listed below are seven high-level steps to consider when formulating and initiating the data collection process.

1. **Identify Those Receiving the Questionnaires**: Using an organizational chart, identify the unit managers, subject matter experts, and key personnel who are qualified to provide required information.

2. **Develop Targeted Questionnaires**: Diverse units within the organization will require different questionnaires based on varying functions. The questionnaires must be tailored to specific critical functions and processes.

3. **Provide Training to Respondents**: Conduct training for those individuals who will be receiving questionnaires to explain the intent, purpose, and expectations of the data collection process. Do not assume respondents understand the document that has been created.

4. **Ensure Timely Completion**: Inform the respondents of the date the questionnaires must be completed and do so with the backing of senior leadership. Open-ended projects tend to stay that way for long periods of time.

5. **Review Responses for Clarity**: Just as it is a mistake to assume respondents will understand documents without training, do not assume those reviewing the submitted documents will understand all of the answers. If those reviewing the questionnaires need clarification for a specific response, seek out the respondent and have it clarified.

6. **Conduct Response Review Meetings**: Response review meetings are a good opportunity to get clarification from the respondents and asking if the respondents need the same for the questionnaires. This holds especially true if a specific set of questions is generating a significant amount of confusion for the respondents.

7. **Compile and Summarize the BIA Data**: Once the data has been collected from the respondents it must compiled into a manageable format and summarized for senior leadership. This also provides an opportunity to identify disparities in responses provided by different individuals within the same organizational units.

BIA Data Collection (Part II)

There are several proven strategies to ensure the data collection process proceeds as smoothly as possible. For example, create a targeted questionnaire for one specific organizational unit and distribute it to the chosen respondents. Once they have been developed and tested in a single unit, distribute them to all appropriate business units. This allows for the questionnaire to be edited and clarified prior to mass distribution. The methods by which questionnaires are developed will change from entity to entity based on organizational needs and context. Listed below are six high-level strategies to consider when streamlining the data collection process.

1. Explain How the BIA Helps all Departments
2. Include a Copy of Executive Support in Writing
3. Request Senior Leadership "Encourage" Respondents
4. Provide Printed Instructions with Questionnaires
5. Provide Examples of Answer Formats
6. Set a Hard Deadline for Completion

Assumption and Exception Workflow

There will be occasions in which senior leadership will ask the BIA project manager to make exceptions or assumptions. To prevent the possibility these requests will reflect poorly on the project manager later, it is advisable to establish a procedure by which those exceptions and assumptions are received and incorporated into the project. This formal procedure will document decisions and validate the acceptance of risk by senior leadership. Exception and assumption procedures will change from entity to entity based on organizational needs and context. Listed below are five general steps to consider when creating this formal process.

1. Submit the Request for a Functional Review
2. Conduct an Assumption Security Review
3. Ensure the Assumption Aligns with the BCP Goals
4. Secure Leadership Approval for the Assumption
5. Document all Leadership Approvals in Writing

Identify Appropriate Respondents

The first step in identifying who should receive the questionnaire is to secure a current copy of the organizational chart. The next step is to identify the critical business units and departments within the organization. Once that has been accomplished, the process of identifying appropriate respondents for the BIA questionnaire can begin. The critical units will change from entity to entity based on organizational needs and context. Listed below are five general guidelines to consider when interacting with potential respondents.

1. **Identify the Leaders of Business Units**: Using a chart of the organizations' unit managers, select the managers to be involved. They will be responsible for ensuring the data collection process is executed within established deadlines.

2. **Leaders are Responsible for Questionnaires**: It is not the function of the project manager to ensure unit staff are completing the questionnaires as required.

3. **Departments Identify Vital Functions**: No one knows the vital function of a specific unit better than those who manage it daily. Although the project manager can provide support and guidance, it will be managers and key personnel of those units that identify critical functions.

4. **Resource Requirements for Functions**: Once the unit managers have identified their critical functions, they must then identify the critical resources that allow those functions to operate. These resources and dependencies may be internal or external contingent upon the function.

5. **Include Critical Suppliers if Possible**: Any suppliers that provide a critical service or product for the function must be identified as well. The suppliers do not need to be unique to the unit, but the must be identified and documented. This could also include technical support for specialized equipment providing a critical service that requires specialized support to sustain its operation.

Often Missed Questions: Personnel

It is important that the project manager not overlook human costs when creating targeted questionnaires. Managers will certainly know the answers to these considerations even though they may be difficult and uncomfortable to address.

1. Employee Morale
2. Employee Turnover (Resignation and Firing)
3. Cost to Hire New Personnel
4. Cost to Train New Personnel
5. Personnel Influence on Social Media

Often Missed Questions: Delayed Costs

Delayed costs are real, tangible, and must be considered when creating the targeted questionnaire. The crisis does not end for an organization immediately after a successful recovery.

1. Wages Paid for no Work
2. Overtime Wages Paid for Recovery Efforts
3. Additional Cost of Financial Credit
4. Devaluation of the Organizations" Stock (if Public)
5. Additional Cost of Insurance

Often Missed Questions: Goodwill

The project manager must ask the right people the right questions and remain aware that biases (discussed previously) may have an impact on responses. It must be stressed to respondents that there are many intangible costs with tangible impacts on their unit.

1. Loss of Shareholder Confidence
2. Loss of Supplier Confidence
3. Loss of Customer Confidence
4. Damage to Organizational Brand and/or Image
5. Loss of Competitive Advantage

Reporting BIA Project Results

Once unit managers have ensured all questionnaires have been returned within the established deadline, the data will be compiled and organized into a hierarchy of targeted reports. The targeted reports will change from entity to entity based on organizational needs and structure. Listed below are five levels of hierarchy to consider when creating targeted reports.

1. Function
2. Work Group
3. Department
4. Organizational Unit
5. Overall Organization

Key Personnel Considerations

When an organization experiences a disaster there will be impacts on key personnel to varying degrees. The impacts can be internal (psychological) or external (geophysical). The project manager may consider the creation of an "Employee Skills Matrix" for the unit leadership. In the event a key employee expected to execute in the BCP is unable to do so, there may be other employees with unknown skill sets available to fill the gap. The key employee considerations will change from entity to entity based on organizational needs and staffing. Listed below are five issues to consider when identifying key personnel.

1. **Stress Created by the Traumatic Event**: If a person has never experienced a traumatic event there is no way to predict their reaction to it. It is quite possible a traumatic event may render someone psychologically inoperable.

2. **Payment, Housing, and Insurance**: The BCP may consider the payment, housing, and insurance needs for its staff, but have the staffs' families been considered? If the organization secures hotel rooms for displaced staff and their families that don't accept pets – and that family has numerous pets they value highly – what choices will they make, and how will that impact the BCP?

3. **Labor and Talent Management Issues**: Does the BCP anticipate the availability of suitable replacements if key personnel leave the organization as a result of the disaster, or as a result of the organizations' response to a disaster?

4. **Directed to Return but Refuses**: If key personnel are ordered to return by the organization to participate in the recovery process, and they refuse to do so due to family issues, what repercussions with these personnel face? If they are key personnel that cannot be terminated because of a critical job function, will non-critical personnel be treated in a similar fashion? If non-critical personnel are not treated equally, how will that impact staffing and morale?

5. **National Guard, Firefighters, and EMS:** Personnel may be members of the National Guard, EMS, or volunteer firefighters without revealing that fact to the organization. These issues can be identified in an "Employee Skills Matrix" and address competing loyalties before a disaster strikes.

Presenting BIA Results to Management

Once the BIA project has been completed, the corresponding reports must be presented to senior leadership. To ensure the highest probability of a successful outcome, preparation and simplicity are the best methods to present compiled results.

Listed below are six presentation tips to consider when making a formal presentation to management.

1. Stay Cool and Start Strong
2. Have a Clear Structure and Objective
3. Know the Stakeholder Audience
4. Anticipate the Tough Questions
5. Make the Message Memorable
6. Ask for What You Need

Slide Presentation Tips

Ideas are judged by how they are presented, and "Death by PowerPoint" should be considered cruel and unusual punishment. It is important for the presented to remember that **they** are the presentation, not the slides. Be bright, be brief, be memorable, and be gone. Listed below are twelve general tips to consider when using slides in support of formal presentations or training.

1. Limit Bullet Points and Text (5-5-5 Rule)
2. Use High-Quality Graphics
3. Use Appropriate Charts and/or Graphs
4. Use Color Well (Conservative Colors)
5. Use Mainstream Fonts
6. Use a Visual Theme but Avoid Templates
7. Use Scripts and Storytelling
8. Use Dark Text on Light Backgrounds
9. Think Outside the Screen (Avoid Slide Fixation)
10. Ask Questions and Engage the Audience
11. Use Voice Modulation and Inflection (no Monotone)
12. Practice the Presentation to Perfection

DOMAIN 02

Overview of The Business Impact Analysis

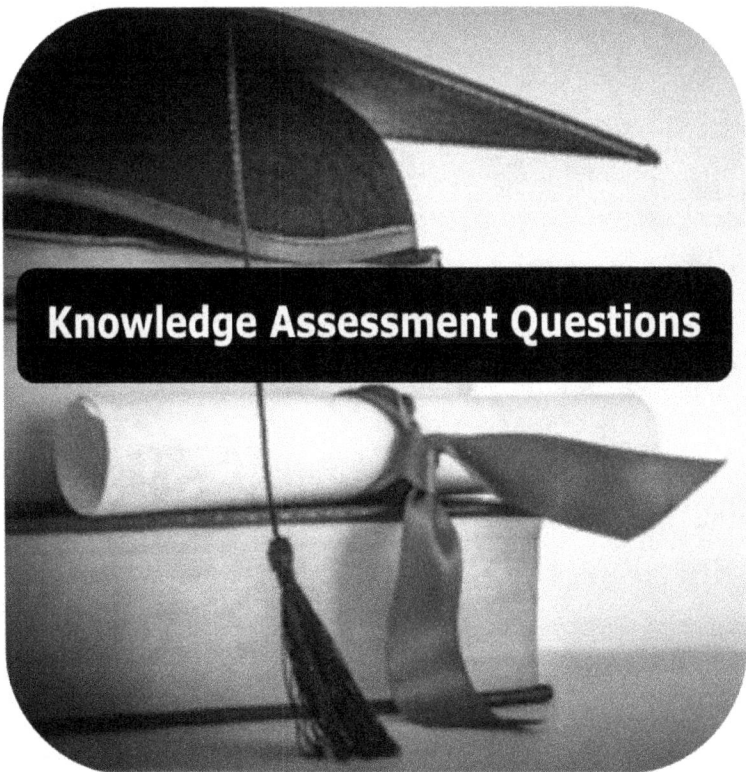

Knowledge Assessment Questions

The following knowledge assessment questions are presented as true / false, multiple choice, and fill-in-the-blank. The correct answers are provided in an Answer Key at the end of the text. These questions may or may not be presented on the actual certification exam.

Domain 02: Knowledge Assessment Questions

1. Which choice below is **not** a direct or indirect benefit of conducting a Business Impact Analysis (BIA)?

A. Identify Critical Functions to Protect

B. Identify Vital Business Records

C. Identify Tangible Costs of Functions

D. Determine Recovery Time Objectives

E. None of the Above

2. A BIA provides many benefits to the organization, many of which are valuable beyond the scope of a business continuity project and allow the BCP Manager to identify _____.

A. Critical Functions to Protect

B. Recovery Time Objectives

C. Vital Business Records

D. Intangible Costs of Functions

E. All of the Above

3. When conducting a Business Impact Analysis (BIA), which choice below would **not** be considered an intangible cost?

A. Reduced Confidence in Marketplace

B. Damage to Image / Brand

C. Products Cannot be Shipped

D. Loss of Faith in Management

E. None of the Above

4. When writing the BIA, _____ would be an example of a tangible financial loss due to a negative impact on a critical business function.

A. Loss of Faith in Senior Management

B. Damage to Image / Brand

C. Reduced Confidence in Marketplace

D. Penalties Imposed by Customers

E. All of the Above

5. Which choice below is **not** a component or characteristic of the Business Impact Analysis (BIA) questionnaire process?

A. Develop Targeted Questionnaires

B. Provide Training to Respondents

C. Ensure Timely Completion

D. Review Responses for Conformity

E. None of the Above

6. When writing the BIA, _____ would be an example of an intangible financial loss due to a negative impact on a critical business function.

A. Services Cannot be Delivered

B. Increased Waste from Spoilage

C. Employee Resignations and Turnover

D. Legal Penalties for Non-Compliance

E. All of the Above

7. Which choice below is **not** a component or characteristic of a formal assumption / exception workflow process?

A. Submit Request for Strategic Review

B. Conduct Assumption Financial Review

C. Ensure Assumption Aligns with BIA

D. Notate All Verbal Exception Approvals

E. All of the Above

8. When selecting a BIA Project Manager, _____ is one of the most important attributes the potential candidate must possess to be successful.

A. Comfortable Moderating Discussions

B. Ivy League University Graduate

C. A Member of Senior Leadership

D. Great Reputation in Community

E. All of the Above

9. Which choice below is **not** a characteristic of selecting questionnaire recipients during a Business Impact Analysis (BIA)?

A. Identify Departments / Business Units

B. Senior Leadership Identifies Vital Functions

C. Resource Requirements for Functions

D. Include Critical Suppliers if Possible

E. None of the Above

10. _____ is a topic that is often overlooked by BCP Managers who do not consider "human costs" when creating BIA questionnaires.

A. Employee Benefits

B. Employee Morale

C. Employee Salary

D. Employee Promotions

E. All of the Above

11. Which choice below is **not** a characteristic of potential delayed costs when conducting a Business Impact Analysis (BIA)?

A. Overtime Wages for Recovery

B. Additional Cost of Credit

C. Devaluation of Stock (Public)

D. Decreased Revenue from Lost Sales

E. None of the Above

12. When a presenter uses slides during a formal presentation, he or she should _____ to ensure the highest probability of a successful outcome.

A. Use a Standard Template

B. Use Animated Graphics

C. Limit Bullet Points and Text

D. Use Creative Fonts

E. All of the Above

13. A Business Inventory Analysis (BIA) provides many benefits to the organization, many of which are valuable beyond the scope of a strategic business plan.

1. True

2. False

14. Intangible costs due to the loss of a vital business function can be more difficult to identify but are no less damaging.

1. True

2. False

15. A well-run Business Impact Analysis (BIA) will generate good press for the overall disaster recovery planning project from the business' public customer base.

1. True

2. False

16. Once the Business Impact Analysis (BIA) questionnaires have been developed and tested in a single unit, distribute them to all appropriate business units.

1. True

2. False

17. Check salary data and key job skills for all selected respondents to help ensure timely completion of the Business Impact Analysis (BIA) questionnaire.

1. True

2. False

18. When using the Business Impact Analysis (BIA) questionnaire ensure you ask the right people the right questions; there are many intangible costs with tangible consequences.

1. True

2. False

DOMAIN 03

Selection of
Risk Management Frameworks

Risk Management: Key Definitions

Risk:

A probability or threat of damage, injury, liability, loss, or any other negative occurrence that is caused by external or internal vulnerabilities, and that may be mitigated through preemptive action.

Vulnerability:

The degree to which people, property, resources, systems, and cultural, economic, environmental, and social activity is susceptible to harm, degradation, or destruction on being exposed to a hostile agent or factor.

Likelihood:

The probability of an events or situations taking place that have a reasonable probability of occurring but are not definite or may be influenced by factors not yet observed or measured.

Risk Sensitivity:

A relative measurement of a resources' tolerance for risk exposures, independent of any threat or vulnerability.

Risk Analysis:

The process of identifying and analyzing potential issues that could negatively impact key business initiatives or critical projects in order to help organizations avoid or mitigate those risks.

Risk Assessment:

The evaluation and estimation of the levels of risks involved in a situation, their comparison against benchmarks or standards, and determination of the probable severity of their impact.

Risk Appetite:

The level of risk that an organization is prepared to accept in pursuit of its objectives, and before action is deemed necessary to reduce the risk.

Residual Risk:

The amount of risk or danger associated with an action or event remaining after natural or inherent risks have been mitigated by risk controls.

The Threat Landscape

The threat landscape faced by Information Security professions is vast, varied, and growing exponentially in response to advances in technology. Additionally, the complexity of IoT is increasing the attack surface and poses a wide variety of unique risks. Threats will change from entity to entity based on technology assets and functionalities. Listed below are five categories of threats typically considered by BCP managers.

1. Physical and Natural Events
2. Loss of Essential Services
3. Compromise of Information
4. Unauthorized Actions
5. Compromise of Functions

The Key Attributes of Risk

They key attributes of risk are those elements BCP managers must take into consideration when crafting a risk management program. All attributes influence risk – and each other – simultaneously.

Attributes of risk will change from entity to entity based on technology assets and functionalities. Listed below are eight attributes typically considered by BCP managers when developing risk management programs and processes.

1. Warning
2. Scope
3. Predictability
4. Time of Day
5. Time of Week
6. Impact
7. Likelihood
8. Capability

The 5 Layers of Risk

Think of risk in terms of concentric circles, with external risk being the farthest from the center. Remember the influences of the attributes of risk; mentally layering risk helps to prioritize solutions. Listed below are five layers of risk typically considered by BCP managers when developing risk management programs and processes.

1. External Risk
2. Facility-Wide Risk
3. Data Systems Risk
4. Unit and Department Risk
5. Proximity Risk (Immediately Observable)

Risk Management Program Development

Developing a risk management program is not complicated, but it is complex insofar as there are many moving parts to consider. As each component is considered, the BCP manager must remain aware of the focus and details of implementation. This focus will help to ensure program development stays within the boundaries of realistic expectations. Listed below are six high-level components typically considered by BCP managers when designing a risk management program.

Domain 03: *Selection of Risk Management Frameworks*

1. Context and Purpose of the Program
2. Scope, Charter, and Methodology
3. Authority, Structure, and Reporting
4. Asset Identification and Classification
5. Risk Management Objectives
6. Creation of the Implementation Team

Risk Management Process

The ability effectively manage risk is contingent upon a successful risk assessment and analysis process. This effort does not have to be created from scratch; there are numerous frameworks available to the BCP manager to support this mission. Listed below are five high-level components typically considered by BCP managers when drafting a risk management process for their organization.

1. Understand the Potential Threats
2. Determine the Existing Vulnerabilities
3. Determine if Risk Levels are Acceptable
4. Assess the Risk Mitigation Options
5. Review the Effectiveness of Implemented Controls

Risk Management Procedure

The risk management procedure is an ongoing and continual process conducted for every critical asset and process identified within the organization. As the organization evolves and changes, so too will the processes in place to manage new risks. Listed below are five high-level steps in the risk management procedure that tend to stay constant within a changing environment.

1. Identify Information Assets and Their Value
2. Perform a Risk Assessment
3. Determine the Risk Treatment and/or Response
4. Accept or Reject the Residual Risk
5. Monitor the Risk and Communicate Results

Conducting an Asset Inventory

To protect any asset within an organization, the BCP manager must know the asset exists. An asset inventory is a comprehensive list of critical assets that organization must protect in order to maintain its vital functions and processes. This is important information for the technical BCP that is typically kept in both the BCP and the asset location. The structure of the asset inventory will change from entity to entity based on the type of assets and criticality. Listed below are six categories of information typically considered when creating an inventory.

1. System Type and Version
2. Installed Software (Including Version)
3. Name and/or Title of the Resource Owner
4. Physical and Logical Location
5. Logical Network Addressing
6. Vendor Support Information

Creating an Asset Resource Profile

An asset resource profile is created for each asset listed on the asset inventory and identifies where and how it fits within the risk management strategy. It is supporting information used for risk mitigation efforts that is attached to the inventory documentation. Listed below are six categories of information typically considered when creating a resource profile.

1. General System Description
2. Functions and Features
3. Information / Data Classification
4. Criticality to the Organization
5. Applicable Compliance Regulations
6. Identified User Community

Asset Valuation

Determining the value of an asset can be challenging, as many tangible and intangible factors must be taken into consideration.

Regardless of the challenging nature of this task, this valuation should be included with the asset inventory and resource profile documentation. The valuation methodology will change from entity to entity based on organizational structure and needs. Listed below are five high-level criteria typically considered when conducting an asset valuation.

1. Criticality and/or Sensitivity
2. Cost to Replace
3. Loss of Revenue
4. Legal and/or Regulatory Sanctions
5. Brand Image and/or Reputational Value

Risk Analysis Methodologies

There are numerous frameworks available to the BCP manager, both technical and non-technical, that can serve as a guideline for the development of risk management procedures and programs. There is no "one size fits all" perfect solution; these models should be adapted and utilized based on specific organizational culture and needs. Listed below are four methodologies that have gained widespread appeal and acceptance: OCTAVE Allegro, FRAAP, FAIR, and the NIST RMF. This list is not meant to be all-inclusive.

1. **OCTAVE Allegro**: The *Operationally Critical Threat, Asset, and Vulnerability Evaluation* uses three phases, and a highly detailed questionnaire to assist in identifying risk. First, an asset-based threat profile is determined. Next, vulnerabilities and exploitation methodologies are identified. Finally, risks and potential mitigation strategies are identified using this information. This methodology is best suited for small projects and one-time assessments.

2. **FRAAP**: The *Facilitated Risk Analysis and Assessment Process* uses subject matter experts and a streamlined approach to conduct risk analysis for project-level assessments. Interdisciplinary experts, led by a facilitator, meet for 4 to 8 hours to conduct the analysis. This method encourages collaboration and can general a final report in just a few days. FRAAP is also easily adaptable into other risk assessment methodologies.

3. **FAIR**: The *Factor Analysis of Information Risk* is based on two factors to measure risk: Loss Event Frequency (LEF) and Probable Loss Magnitude (PLM). Using measurable statistics of frequency, capability, and control strength it creates a six-level risk exposure table that can be used as the source of mitigation strategies. This is a detailed quantitative and probabilistic analysis method best suited for larger and more advanced projects.

4. **NIST RMF**: *The National Institute of Standards and Technology Risk Management Framework* is a real-time continuous monitoring risk analysis methodology. It supports the use of automated tools (such as SIEM) to inform risk decisions, integration with system architecture, and integration at all levels of the System Development Life Cycle. It also establishes a model for the accountability of security controls. The NIST RMF uses a six-step, high-level approach that consists of the following categories:

   a. **Categorize**: System Information
   b. **Select**: Security Controls
   c. **Implement**: Security Controls
   d. **Assess**: Security Controls
   e. **Authorize**: Information System
   f. **Monitor**: Security Controls

Vulnerability Assessment ≠ Risk Assessment

A *vulnerability assessment* is a useful tool to identify potential weaknesses that may be visible to threat sources, but it is not the same as a risk assessment. Listed below are five facts about vulnerability that distinguishes it from risk.

1. Used to Identify Potential System Weaknesses
2. Based on Rules, Known Exploits, and Parameters
3. Not all Vulnerabilities Pose Risks
4. One Vulnerability can Pose Many Risks
5. A Component of the Risk Assessment Process

Risk Assessment ≠ Vulnerability Assessment

A *risk assessment* is a useful tool to evaluate risk and develop mitigation strategies that align with organizational processes, but it is not the same as a vulnerability assessment. Listed below are five facts about risk assessment that distinguishes it from vulnerability assessment.

1. Based on Category of Information and/or Data
2. Accounts for System Architecture
3. Accounts for Existing Security Controls
4. Based on Capability, Likelihood, and Impact
5. Provides a Multi-Dimensional View of the Environment

Manufactured Risks: Cost Estimate Challenges

Risk can be avoided, assumed, transferred, and mitigated but it cannot be removed entirely. Nowhere is this more apparent than with manufactured risks. These risks are difficult to quantify and qualify, the BCP manager must be aware that they exist even if they cannot be controlled. Listed below are five examples of these risks that expose many organizations to potential disasters daily.

1. **Industrial Sites**: Toxic Chemical Tanks
2. **Airports**: Organization in a Flight Path
3. **Fires**: Water and Smoke Damage Impacts
4. **Pipelines**: Combustible Gas and/or Fuels
5. **Infrastructure**: Fragility and/or Dependencies

DOMAIN 03

Selection of
Risk Management Frameworks

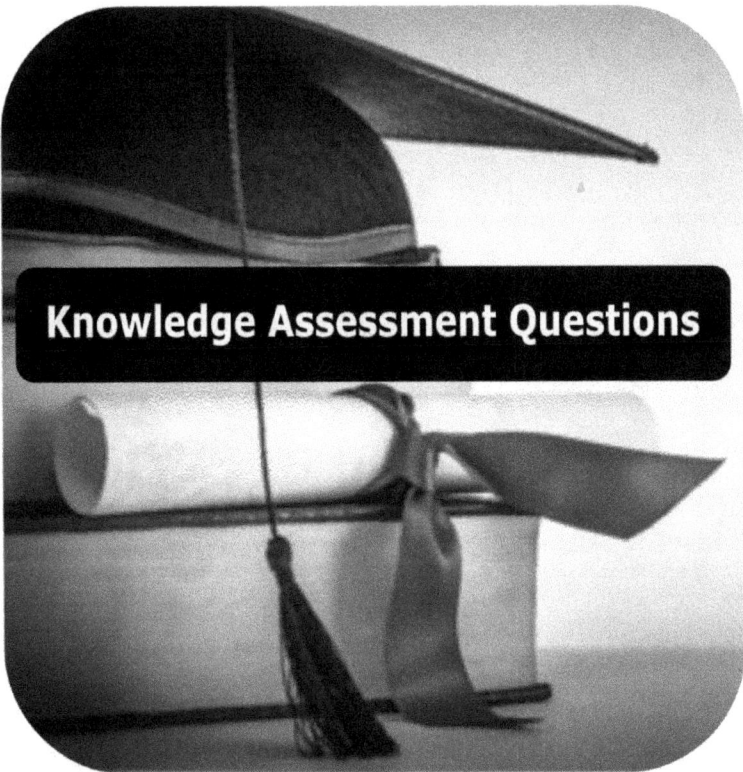

Knowledge Assessment Questions

The following knowledge assessment questions are presented as true / false, multiple choice, and fill-in-the-blank. The correct answers are provided in an Answer Key at the end of the text. These questions may or may not be presented on the actual certification exam.

Domain 03: Knowledge Assessment Questions

1. Which choice below is **not** a characteristic of the threat landscape posed by the "Internet of Things" (IoT)?

A. Loss of Essential Services

B. Compromise of Information

C. Unauthorized Actions

D. Compromise of Functions

E. None of the Above

2. _____ is a well-established and widely used risk management framework that is best suited for small projects and one-time assessments.

A. NIST RMF

B. FAIR

C. FRAAP

D. OCTAVE Allegro

E. All of the Above

3. *"The process of identifying and analyzing potential issues that could negatively impact key business initiatives or critical projects in order to help organizations avoid or mitigate those risks."*

A. Risk Assessment

B. Risk

C. Risk Analysis

D. Residual Risk

E. Vulnerability

4. _____ is a well-established and widely used risk management framework with a style that is easily adaptable to other analysis methods.

A. NIST RMF

B. FAIR

C. FRAAP

D. OCTAVE Allegro

E. All of the Above

5. Which choice below is **not** a primary goal or objective when implementing the risk management process?

A. Understand Potential Threats

B. Determine if Risk Levels are Acceptable

C. Assess Risk Mitigation Options

D. Operate Within Financial Constraints

E. None of the Above

6. _____ is a well-established and widely used risk management framework that is a detailed quantitative and probabilistic analysis method.

A. NIST RMF

B. FAIR

C. FRAAP

D. OCTAVE Allegro

E. All of the Above

7. Which choice below is a characteristic or component of conducting a successful asset inventory in support of a Business Continuity Plan (BCP)?

A. System Type and Version

B. Physical and Logical Location

C. Logical Network Addressing

D. Vendor Support Information

E. All of the Above

8. _____ is a well-established and widely used risk management framework consisting of six steps and replaces the "Certification and Accreditation" model.

A. NIST RMF

B. FAIR

C. FRAAP

D. OCTAVE Allegro

E. All of the Above

9. Which choice below is **not** a basic consideration when conducting an asset valuation in support of a Business Continuity Plan (BCP)?

A. Criticality and/or Sensitivity

B. Employee Skill Sets

C. Cost to Replace

D. Loss of Revenue

E. None of the Above

10. When attempting to identify manufactured risks such as _____, the BCP Manager must emphasize the need to be aware of the risks even if they cannot be controlled.

A. Temperature in Server Area

B. Wiring in Electrical Closet

C. Property Perimeter Fencing

D. Underground Gas Pipelines

E. All of the Above

11. Which choice below is **not** a component, characteristic, or objective of conducting a vulnerability assessment?

A. Identify Potential System Weaknesses

B. Based on Rules / Known Exploits

C. A Part of the Risk Assessment Process

D. Based on Capability, Likelihood, Impact

E. None of the Above

12. The six steps associated with the NIST Risk Management Framework are Categorize, Select, Implement, _____, Authorize, and Monitor.

A. Appraise

B. Audit

C. Assess

D. Analyze

E. All of the Above

13. Not all third-party service providers can be audited, but for those that can the audit requirement should be considered after the Service Level Agreement (SLA) is renewed.

1. True

2. False

14. When identifying and predicting the costs of manufactured risks, document the fact the risks exist even if they cannot be controlled or mitigated.

1. True

2. False

15. A vulnerability assessment is a useful tool to ensure risk evaluation and mitigation align with business and organizational needs.

1. True

2. False

16. Creating an Asset Resource Profile provides confidential information for risk mitigation; document the resource profile on an asset inventory page.

1. True

2. False

17. Asset inventories are optional information for the Administrative Continuity Plan (BCP) that is typically kept in both the BCP and a back-up storage location.

1. True

2. False

18. Adapt and utilize established Risk Management reference models based on organizational culture and specific needs.

1. True

2. False

Qualitative and Quantitative Analysis Strategies

Overview: Qualitative Analysis

Qualitative Analysis:
Examination and evaluation of non-measurable data using subjective judgement and non-quantifiable methods.

Most *qualitative analysis* approaches use a relative scale to rate risk exposures based on a set of predefined criteria for each level. Like all analysis methodologies it has strengths and weaknesses. Its strength lies in affording BCP managers a way to measure risks that cannot be measured quantitatively and map this risk to an end exposure value. However, this method does have limitations and weaknesses. Listed below are three primary shortcomings to consider when using this method for evaluating risks.

1. It Relies Heavily on the Knowledge of the Assessor
2. It is Subjective and Prone to Inaccuracies
3. It Uses a Scale Based on Descriptive Criteria

Defining Severity

The severity rating used in the qualitative analysis method is meant to describe the scope of the exposure, not list all the potential consequences. It is asset agnostic and measures the magnitude of exploiting a weakness contingent upon it impact on the CIA (or CIAA) Triad. The severity is rated by the degree of disruption based on the time and scope of the resources that are affected. Although there can be any number of levels in a severity rating, the rating scales are typically low, medium, and high.

Data Availability Severity

Developing qualitative risk scales for data availability severity are a great opportunity to design a business focus directly into the risk model. After all, an organization that cannot access or disseminate its data cannot execute its mission. The goal for the BCP manager is to create a clear set of criteria for each level of severity with visible distinctions between each level.

If the distinctions between the levels proves to be obscure of confusing, the severity scales can be revised for clarity. Data severity scales will change from entity to entity based on organizational needs and context. Listed below are four metrics typically considered by BCP managers when creating these scales.

1. Impact on External Services
2. Impact on Internal Processes
3. Degradation of Overall Performance
4. Length of time of the Disruption

Data Integrity Severity

Data integrity severity will focus primarily on unauthorized or unintended access to create, read, update, or delete data ("CRUD"). Additionally, the severity scales will consider the varying degrees of unauthorized or unintended access. Integrity severity scales will change from entity to entity based on organizational needs and context. Listed below are three examples of how varying degrees of severity can be used by the BCP manager to create these qualitative scales.

1. **Low**:   May Indirectly Contribute to Integrity Issues
2. **Medium**:   May Allow Limited Unauthorized Access
3. **High**:   May Allow Unrestricted Unauthorized Access

Questions for Estimating Severity

Estimating severity using a qualitative analysis method may prove to be challenging for BCP managers. If difficulty exists qualifying the severity of a vulnerability, many useful questions can be asked to improve clarity. Listed below are six examples of questions that can be asked by the BCP manager to create these scales.

1. What is the Scope of Severity Post-Exploitation?
2. What is the Degree of Service Shutdown?
3. Will its Form be Executable Code or Arbitrary Functions?
4. Will Accessed Data Help Exploit Other Systems?
5. Will the Impact be Internal or External?
6. Are These Unique or Aggregated Threats?

Questions for Estimating Likelihood

Estimating likelihood using a qualitative analysis method can pose similar challenges for BCP managers as when estimating severity. As with estimating severity, if difficulty exists qualifying the threat/vulnerability pairs, many useful questions can be asked to improve clarity. The BCP manager must also be aware that it is not uncommon to confuse the contributing factors impacting the likelihood and severity of the threat/vulnerability pairs. Listed below are eleven examples of questions typically asked by the BCP manager to create these scales.

1. What is the Size and/or Population of the Threat Universe?
2. Is There a Location Requirement for Exposure?
3. Is There Available Information About the Exploit?
4. What Skill Level is Required to Execute the Exploit?
5. How Attractive is the Target to Malicious Actors?
6. Has the Exploit Been Executed in the Past?
7. Is the Exploit Applicable in the Current Environment?
8. Is an AV, IDS, or IPS Signature Available?
9. Is Authentication Required for the Exploit?
10. What is the Impact on Servers and/or Endpoints?
11. Is the Vulnerability Widely Deployed?

Challenges of Quantitative Analysis

Quantitative Analysis:
*The process of collecting and evaluating
measurable and verifiable data in
order to understand the condition
and performance of a business.*

Quantitative analysis methods are considered to be more exact than their qualitative counterparts insofar as they are an object means to evaluate measurable and verifiable data. Although this can be true in many situations, this method still has challenges. Many quantitative models have been proposed over the years with very complex equations for calculating risk, but none have been the "silver bullet" for BCP managers. Listed below are six examples challenges typically faced when using this method.

1. **Lack of Accessible Historical Data**: This method relies on historical data to create benchmarks and predict trends. If such data does not exist or is not accessible, originating assumptions will be speculative.

2. **Reliance on Extremely Accurate Data**: If historical data is available and accessible it must also be extremely accurate for the analysis to yield effective results.

3. **Requires Significant Time to Analyze**: Large datasets take a significant amount of time to analyze and may not be practical for short-term needs. Even with the support of machine learning systems, human participation to evaluate results cannot be avoided.

4. **Reluctance to Share Vital Information**: Accurate historical data may be available and accessible to members of a specific organization, but few organizations are inclined to share their vital information with external entities. This can also occur within a single organization if the culture is compartmentalized.

5. **Anonymous Surveys are Rarely Honest**: In the absence of accurate historical data, anonymous questionnaires may be used to collected needed information (Delphi Method). In many cases respondents will not provide answers that are truthful for fear their responses will be traced back to them.

6. **Data is Skewed to Specific Industries**: Large studies generating a high volume of statistics may provide useful information but tend to be skewed to the specific industries that sponsored or commissioned the study.

Asset Value Considerations

The valuation of assets, both tangible and intangible, is a critical component of risk assessment, analysis, and management. The assessment must transcend line-item numbers as the asset value can extend well beyond the actual cost.

Asset value considerations will change from entity to entity based on organizational needs and context. Listed below are six questions typically asked by the BCP manager to determine the true value of an organizational asset.

1. What is the Actual Cost of the Asset?
2. What is the Cost to Replace if it is a Legacy Asset?
3. What is the Functional Value to the Organization?
4. Do any Operational Dependencies Exist?
5. What are the Assets' Compliance Requirements?
6. What is the Criticality of the Assets' Data?

Calculating SLE and ALE

The BCP manager can use qualitative analysis to determine asset value by calculating Single Loss Expectancy and Annualized Loss Expectancy for each critical asset. Review the definitions below to become familiar with the related terms listed below.

Exposure Factor (EF):

The subjective, potential percentage of loss to a particular asset if a specific threat occurs.

Single Loss Expectancy (SLE):

The monetary value expected from the one-time occurrence of a risk on an asset.

Annual Rate of Occurrence (ARO):

An estimated probability of frequency of an occurrence of a risk on an asset in a given year.

Annualized Loss Expectancy (ALE):

The monetary value expected from an occurrence of a risk on an asset distributed over a given period of time.

Calculating Annualized Rate of Occurrence (ARO)

The ARO is a method for calculating probability over time and is one of the components used in the ALE equation. To determine ARO divide the number of years by the yearly likelihood of an occurrence as shown is the table below.

1 Year	1/1	**1.0**		6 Years	1/6	**.17**
2 Years	1/2	**0.5**		7 Years	1/7	**.14**
3 Years	1/3	**.33**		8 Years	1/8	**.13**
4 Years	1/4	**.25**		9 Years	1/9	**.11**
5 Years	1/5	**0.2**		10 Years	1/10	**0.1**

Calculating Single Loss Expectancy (SLE)

To calculate SLE, multiply the Asset Value by the Exposure Factor. This operation is expressed as AV x EF = _____ . This answers the question, "*What is the assets' value and what percentage of the value will be impacted by an occurrence?*" For example, an asset with a value of $5,000 that has a 75% exposure will have a SLE of $3,750 (5,000 x .75 = $3,750). The EF exists because an occurrence may not have a 100% impact on a given asset.

Calculating Annualized Loss Expectancy (ALE)

To calculate ALE, multiply the Single Loss Expectancy by the Annual Rate of Occurrence. This operation is expressed as SLE x ARO = _____ . This answers the question, "*What is the yearly cost of an occurrence on an asset if the cost is distributed over a given number of years?*" Using the numbers from the example above, an asset with a SLE of $3,750 ($5,000 x 75%) would have an ALE of $1,875 ($3.750 x .5) if the asset was exposed to an occurrence, and the losses from that occurrence were distributed over a two-year period. This qualitative method can be used with any asset, and Exposure Factor, and any Annual Rate of Occurrence. However, the BCP manager must be aware that the costs generated by this method may be underreported due to the assets' data and delayed costs.

Domain 04: *Qualitative and Quantitative Analysis Strategies*

To effectively calculate the true ALE of a given asset other factors must be taken into consideration. Still using the numbers from the examples above, assume the asset was a server used for email. The ALE was calculated as $1,875. Now assume the asset is a database server in a hospital containing *Personally Identifiable Information* (PII) and *Personal Healthcare Information* (PHI). Is the $1,875 calculation for ALE still correct? Listed below are a few questions to consider when answering that question.

1. What is the average cost per file for a data breach?
2. What are the regulatory fines for a data breach?
3. What are the legal costs arising from civil litigation?
4. What is the cost to provide credit reporting for victims?

Asset Value: The Broader Picture

The Ponemon Institute (https://www.ponemon.org), a respected source of data statistics, estimates that the average cost per file in 2018 compromised in a breach was $158. The regulatory fines for a data breach vary between industry sectors but can be obtained from the regulatory agencies themselves. The legal costs for civil litigation cannot be quantitatively determined, but a wide variety of respected source provide accurate historical data and trends. The typical annual cost for credit monitoring and reporting is $99. Although only two values are definitely known a new ALE can be calculated that presents a very different picture.

Using the ALE value from the examples above, calculate the knowable cost of a $5,000 (AV) database server with a 75% exposure factor (EF) containing 10,000 customer files with PII. The original ALE of $1,875 would still be accurate but the values listed below must now be added.

1. **Files Lost:**   7,500 (10,000 x .75)
2. **File Cost:** $1,185,000 (7,500 x $158)
3. **Reporting:** $742, 500 (7,500 x $99)
4. **Litigation:**   Unknown
5. **Fines:**   Unknown
6. **Known Total:**   **$1,927,500** (not $1,875)

Domain 04: *Qualitative and Quantitative Analysis Strategies*

Many organizations take a line-item approach to calculating the value of assets and, for the majority of circumstances, that approach is rational. Unfortunately it can present an inaccurate assessment for senior leadership and an underfunded program for a BCP manager. Both the senior leadership and the BCP manager will be unprepared and ill-prepared in the event a response to a disaster is required.

Respected Sources of Statistics

The BCP manager has access to respected sources of statistical data that will provide information to "fill in the blanks" and create more accurate assessments for senior leadership. Listed below are a few sources which are discussed in this course, but this is by no means meant to be an all-inclusive list.

The Ponemon Institute
https://www.ponemon.org

Common Vulnerabilities and Exposures (CVE)
https://cve.mitre.org

Federal Bureau of Investigation (FBI)
https://www.fbi.gov/investigate/cyber

The OWASP Foundation
https://www.owasp.org

DOMAIN 04

Qualitative and Quantitative Analysis Strategies

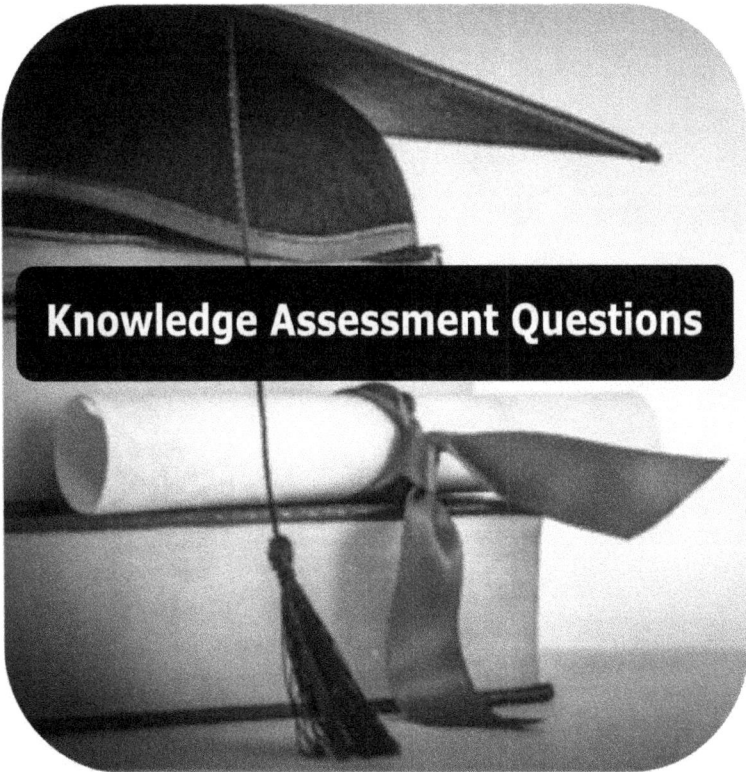

The following knowledge assessment questions are presented as true / false, multiple choice, and fill-in-the-blank. The correct answers are provided in an Answer Key at the end of the text. These questions may or may not be presented on the actual certification exam.

Domain 04: Knowledge Assessment Questions

1. Which choice below is **not** the general characteristics and/or components of a qualitative analysis?

A. Objective and Accurate Analysis

B. Relies on Knowledge of Assessor

C. Scale Based on Descriptive Criteria

D. Maps to End Risk Exposure Value

E. None of the Above

2. _____ can be defined as the expected monetary loss for an asset due to a risk over a one-year period.

A. Annualized Rate of Occurrence

B. Single Loss Expectancy

C. Asset Valuation

D. Annualized Loss Expectancy

E. None of the Above

3. Which choice below is **not** a consideration or objective when attempting to determine the severity of impact on data availability?

A. Impact on External Services

B. Impact on Internal Processes

C. Degradation of Performance

D. Degrees of Unauthorized Access

E. None of the Above

4. _____ can be defined as the probability that a risk will occur in a particular year.

A. Annualized Rate of Occurrence

B. Single Loss Expectancy

C. Asset Valuation

D. Annualized Loss Expectancy

E. None of the Above

5. Which choice below is **not** a consideration or question to be asked when attempting to determine the severity of a specific vulnerability?

A. What is the Scope After Exploitation?

B. Internal or External Impact?

C. How Attractive is the Target?

D. Are Threats Unique or Aggregated?

E. None of the Above

6. _____ can be defined as the monetary value expected from the occurrence of a risk on an asset.

A. Annualized Rate of Occurrence

B. Single Loss Expectancy

C. Asset Valuation

D. Annualized Loss Expectancy

E. None of the Above

7. Which choice below is **not** a challenge to be overcome when attempting to conduct a quantitative analysis?

A. Data Standardized for All Industries

B. Requires Significant Time to Analyze

C. Anonymous Surveys Rarely Honest

D. Lack of Accessible Historical Data

E. All of the Above

8. _____ can be defined as the process of determining the fair market or present value of assets.

A. Annualized Rate of Occurrence

B. Single Loss Expectancy

C. Asset Valuation

D. Annualized Loss Expectancy

E. None of the Above

9. Which choice below is a consideration or question to be asked when attempting to determine the actual value of an asset?

A. Actual Cost of Asset

B. Criticality of Asset Data

C. Functional Value to Business

D. Existing Operational Dependencies

E. All of the Above

10. Most _____ analysis approaches use a relative scale to rate risk exposures based on a set of predefined criteria for each level.

A. Accepted

B. Quantitative

C. Predictive

D. Qualitative

E. None of the Above

11. Which choice below is a general characteristic and/or component which exist when defining levels of severity?

A. Severity Level is Asset Agnostic

B. Contingent Upon Impact on CIAA

C. Rated by Degree of Disruption

D. Scale: Low, Moderate, and High

E. All of the Above

12. A BCP Manager concerned with _____ will focus primarily on unauthorized or unintended access to create, read, update, or delete data ("CRUD").

A. Confidentiality Severity

B. Availability Severity

C. Integrity Severity

D. Accountability Severity

E. None of the Above

13. Most qualitative analysis approaches use a relative scale to rate risk exposures based on a set of predefined criteria for each level.

1. True
2. False

14. Developing qualitative risk scales are a great opportunity to design a security focus directly into the risk model.

1. True
2. False

15. If you are having trouble qualifying the severity of a vulnerability, many useful questions can be asked to improve clarity.

1. True
2. False

16. Many quantitative analysis models have been proposed over the years with complex equations for calculating vulnerabilities.

1. True
2. False

17. Annualized Rate of Occurrence (ARO): calculate probability over time by dividing one year by the predicted likelihood of the event in question.

1. True
2. False

18. Integrity severity concerns will focus primarily on unauthorized or unintended access to falsify, steal, or embezzle data.

1. True
2. False

DOMAIN 05

Implementing the
5 Levels of BCP Testing

Writing a Testing Strategy

To maximize the benefit to the organization while minimizing costs, develop a written testing strategy for the BCP. The testing strategy will be a written document in the Administrative BCP describing the types and frequency of testing. The testing strategy will have formal approval of senior leadership (as do all documents in the Administrative BCP) which serves to establish a higher level of compliance with the plan.

Calendars are typically planned for a span of several years. The BCP manager must consider that organizational units have a variety of "busy seasons" that would make participation difficult. Initiate the testing strategy with an individual plan, then expand it over time to include multiple BCP groupings.

Developing Testing Goals

As with all initiatives related to the BCP, begin setting goals for the testing plan by referring to the BIA. Goals will change from entity to entity based on organizational structure and needs. Listed below are six points relating to testing goals of threats typically considered by BCP managers.

1. **Brief RTO** = Testing is More Frequent
2. **Long RTO** = Testing is Less Frequent
3. Incident Severity can Change Existing RTO's
4. Specific Process RTO's can Differ
5. Critical Processes are Tested Frequently
6. All Participants Must Understand Their Roles

Creating the Testing Team

The best BCP testing results come from a clear explanation of the responsibilities of team members, and training to show them what to do. Listed below are five categories of participants that typically make up a BCP testing team.

1. The Business Continuity Manager
2. The Test Sponsor

3. The Exercise Recorder
4. The Exercise Participants
5. External Non-Organizational Participants

Leading BCP Testing Exercises

Leading a testing exercise takes planning, preparation, and a complete understanding of expected outcomes and goals. Choosing a relevant test scenario can be difficult contingent upon the specific needs of the participants. The scenario should be focused on the type of problem that a specific group of people are likely to face. Test scenarios will change from entity to entity based on organizational structure and needs. Listed below are seven points typically considered by BCP managers who intend to lead testing exercises.

1. Scenarios Reflect Real and Potential Threats
2. Use Risk Analysis and Risk Assumptions in Planning
3. The Expertise of the Coordinator is Critical
4. Create a Detailed Timeline of Events
5. Allocate, Coordinate, and Stage all Resources
6. Establish and Assign Specific Participant Roles
7. Identify and Address Relevant Interdependencies

The Benefits of BCP Testing

An untested plan is nothing more than process documentation. During times of crisis, people tend to react the way they were trained, and perception tends to become the reality. A test that is conducted well and thoroughly can have a positive influence on the participants. Listed below are five benefits that typically result from well-conducted BCP testing exercises.

1. Reveal Plan Errors and/or Incorrect Assumptions
2. Uncover Changes Made Since the Plan was Written
3. Reveal Missing and/or Unnecessary Steps
4. Identify Unknown Contingencies
5. Verify Resource and/or Asset Availability

The 5 Progressions of BCP Testing

The 5 levels of BCP testing allow for incremental improvements over time and a wider variety of testing to be conducted more often. Listed below are five progressions of BCP tests typically conducted by organizations. These tests will be discussed in further detail in the following pages.

1. Checklist Testing
2. Table-Top Testing
3. Structured Walk-Through
4. Parallel Testing
5. Fail-Over Testing (Full Interruption)

Progression 01: Checklist Testing

Checklist testing is the first (and easiest) level of the BCP testing progression. The objective of this test is to create and work through a BCP that is standardized and understood by all of the participants. The administration of this test will change from entity to entity based on testing goals and organizational needs. Listed below are five characteristics typical of this type of test.

1. Required After Significant System Changes are Made
2. Tests Individual IT and Business Processes
3. The First Level of Error-Checking for Plans
4. The Objective is Complete Recovery from Nothing
5. Ensures that the Recovery Plan is Understandable

Progression 02: Table-Top Testing

Table-Top testing is the second level of BCP testing progression. The objective of this test is to train specific team members, identify omissions in the plan, and raise general awareness of the BCP. Listed below are five characteristics typical of this type of test.

1. Initiated as a Simulated Emergency Scenario
2. A Test of the Participants' Decision-Making Processes

    3. Focuses on Analysis, Communication, and Collaboration
    4. Includes Mid-Exercise Problem Injections
    5. Typically Conducted as a Half-Day Exercise

Progression 03: Structured Walk-Through

The *structured walk-through* is the third level of the BCP testing progression. The objective of this test is to focus on specific IT assets and is typically conducted in the environment in which the assets are located. Listed below are five characteristics typical of this type of test.

    1. Tests Multiple Plans in Logical Groupings
    2. Ensures Effective Data Exchange and Communication
    3. Test the Strength of Asset Interdependencies
    4. Can Utilize Disaster Recovery Site Machines and Systems
    5. Beneficial in Determining Realistic RTO's

Progression 04: Parallel Testing

The *parallel test* is the fourth level of the BCP testing progression and tends to be more complex than the first three progressions. The objective of this test is to evaluate the BCP with actual systems at the recovery site without the risk of interrupting the operation of the organization. Listed below are five characteristics typical of this type of test.

    1. Conducted as a Realistic Emergency Scenario
    2. Tests Multiple and Logical Groups of Plans Simultaneously
    3. Includes Key Personnel and Recovery Site Systems
    4. Actions are Conducted at the Disaster Recovery Site
    5. The Exercise Typically Runs for Several Days

Progression 05: Fail-Over Testing

The *fail-over test* (full interruption) is the fifth level of the BCP testing progression and is by far the riskiest of all the BCP test progressions. The objective of this to create a full interruption of the organizations' system to definitively test the BCP.

Domain 05: *Implementing the 5 Levels of BCP Testing*

Listed below are five characteristics typical of this type of test.

1. There is a Full Shutdown of the Primary Location
2. There is a Full Activation of the Secondary Site
3. This Test Creates 100% Confidence in the BCP
4. A Suitable Test for Mature and Redundant Systems
5. The Exercise Typically Runs for Several Days

Potential Testing Scenarios

Realistic testing scenarios based on recent events tend to generate more "buy in" from BCP testing participants. The testing coordinator must also ensure any scenario selected will have relevant and achievable outcomes. The potential testing scenarios will change from entity to entity based on testing goals and the organizations' location and needs. Listed below are four examples of testing scenarios that replicate real-world events.

1. Natural Disasters
2. Civil Crisis and Unrest
3. Geographic Location and Proximity Threats
4. Network and Information Security Threats

Improvisational Exercises

Planned events can create unique opportunities to execute testing scenarios that are relevant to the business operation. It is the BCP managers' responsibility to be aware of these scheduled events to ensure enough time is available to allocate necessary resources and plan the exercise. Listed below are five examples of improvisational testing opportunities that typically exist for most organizations.

1. Scheduled Power Outages (Maintenance or Conservation)
2. Facility Construction Projects
3. Business Unit and/or System Relocation
4. New Facility Acquisition (Pre-Occupancy)
5. Local Government Disaster Drills (Published and Open)

Demonstrating RTO Capability

The RTO for any function or process is typically based on a perceived need identified by an organization. However, that need is not always consistent with the ability to achieve the RTO. BCP tests allow for actual RTO's to be documented and measured under the best and worst of circumstances. BIA estimates are never completely accurate despite best efforts; BCP testing measures written theory against documented reality. It also allows the BCP manager to consider parallel tasking options, reevaluate tasking sequences, and identify (then eliminate) non-essential tasks. This type of analysis will determine if the RTO can be achieved with a more streamlined approach, or if it must be adjusted to reflect more realistic expectations and outcomes.

Debriefing Exercise Participants

Once any progression of BCP testing has been concluded, the next critical step for the BCP manager is to debrief all participants involves with any aspect of the testing. This is a two-way exchange of information between the test facilitators and participants. *This type of debriefing is not restricted to BCP testing alone*. Whenever an incident occurs in the organization that is covered by the BCP, the BCP manager should conduct an after-action review on the next workday after the recovery. The debriefing style and timeframes will change from entity to entity based on the organizations' policy and needs. Listed below are five topics typically included in any BCP test debriefing.

1. **What Happened?** Different participants will have different perceptions contingent upon what role they were assigned. Collecting this information will provide the BCP manager with a holistic view of the testing event in its entirety.

2. **What Should Have Happened?** Each participant assigned a role in the testing scenario knew the expectations going into the exercise, observed what occurred during the test, and will be able to identify any gaps that existed. Collecting this information will provide the BCP manager with an accurate idea of what areas of the plan need to be revisited for improvement.

3. **What Went Well?** Only on the rarest occasions will every objective of a test be missed. Collecting this information will provide the BCP manager with an accurate assessment of the plan items that worked, even if they can be better.

4. **What Did Not Go Well?** This will most likely be the easiest question to answer (in theory) but the most difficult for the test participants to articulate (in reality). Hearing opinions is important, but the BCP manager should stay focused on objective analysis and ensure participants do not engaged in finger-pointing or the "blame game."

5. **What Will We Do Differently?** Although this question is typically answered after all information has been collected, there are some actionable items which will be obvious to all participants immediately after the test ends. This is a good time for the BCP manager to solicit feedback and positive suggestions from everyone involved with the test.

Participant Testing Considerations

When BCP testing outcomes fall short of expectations, especially during high-intensity scenarios, emotions of the participants can increase exponentially both for better and for worse. The BCP manager must be aware of this during the initial debriefing and the days following the test as well. Ignoring the emotions and concerns of test participants will discourage participation in future tests. Listed below are seven suggested guidelines for BCP managers to follow when considering the emotional state of test participants.

1. Praise in Public
2. Criticize in Private
3. Do not Assign Blame to Participants
4. Discovering Gaps is Not Equal to Failure
5. Keep Observations and Analysis Objective
6. Remove Judgment from any Consideration
7. Respect, Acknowledge, and Document Dissenting Opinions

BCP Training and Awareness

Training and awareness are the core of successful BCP testing programs; people will typically act (and react) in the manner they were trained. The training methodologies and mediums will change from entity to entity based on the organizations' policy and needs. Listed below are six typical characteristics incorporated into successful BCP training programs.

1. Identify Clear Training Goals and Outcomes
2. Make the Training Engaging, Fun, and Competitive
3. Focus on Changing Behaviors and Perceptions
4. Strive to Bridge the "Knowledge vs. Action" Gap
5. Tailor Appropriate Training to the Target Audience
6. Solicit Participant Ideas and Encourage Feedback

Benefits of Certifying the BCP

Third-party certification of BCP plans is not a requirement, but it does have benefits that may justify this expense to the organization. BCP testing can be unintentionally structured to focus on a plans' strengths while glossing over weaknesses; professional certification addresses this issue using objective third parties.

Examples of certification programs include ITIL, COBIT, ISO, and CMMI and are typically selected based on the organizations' industry and compliance needs. Listed below are five potential benefits that third-party certifications may provide to a BCP program.

1. Objective External Reviews can Reveal Weaknesses
2. Process Ensures Alignment with Best Practices
3. Certification Provides a Higher Degree of Confidence
4. Certification Provides a Higher Degree of Credibility
5. Certification can Fulfill a Responsibility to Stakeholders

Implementing the 5 Levels of BCP Testing

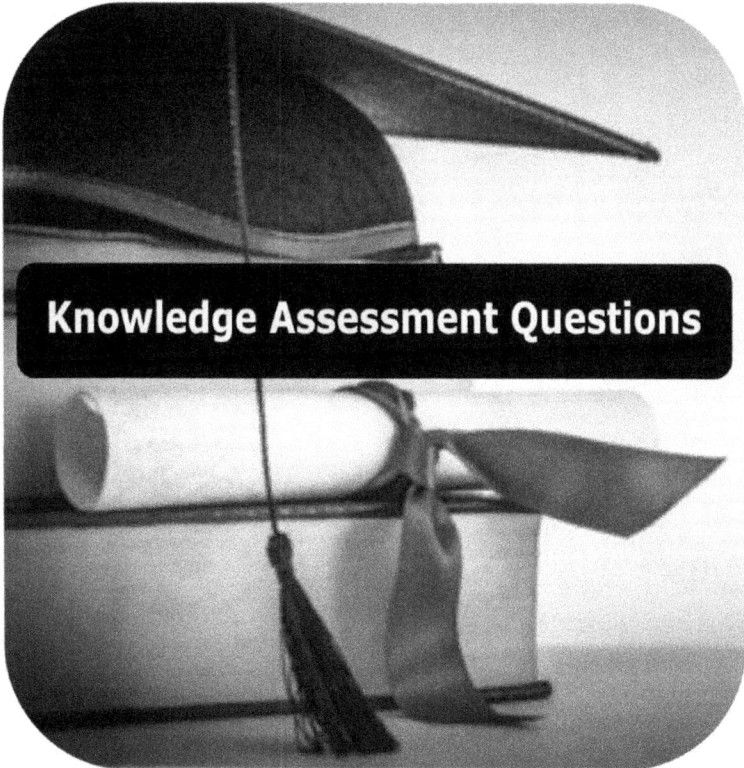

The following knowledge assessment questions are presented as true / false, multiple choice, and fill-in-the-blank. The correct answers are provided in an Answer Key at the end of the text. These questions may or may not be presented on the actual certification exam.

Domain 05: Knowledge Assessment Questions

1. Which choice below is **not** a characteristic or objective of documenting a testing strategy for the Business Continuity Plan (BCP)?

A. Describes Type / Frequency of Testing

B. Improvisational Testing Creates Compliance

C. Begin with Individual Plan

D. Calendar Planned for Several Years

E. None of the Above

2. The objective of a _____ is to create and work through a BCP that is standardized and understood by all participants.

A. Fail-Over Test

B. Parallel Test

C. Checklist Test

D. Table-Top Test

E. None of the Above

3. Which choice below is a characteristic that must be considered when creating strategies to test Recovery Time Objectives (RTO's)?

A. Brief RTO = Testing Less Frequent

B. Specific Process RTO Remain Constant

C. All Participants Understand Roles

D. Long RTO = Testing More Frequent

E. All of the Above

4. The objective of a _____ is to train specific team members, identify omissions, and raise general awareness of the BCP.

A. Fail-Over Test

B. Parallel Test

C. Checklist Test

D. Table-Top Test

E. None of the Above

5. Which choice below is **not** a primary benefit to be considered when testing the Business Continuity Plan (BCP)?

A. Testing Deficiencies Increase BCP Budget

B. Reveal Plan Errors / Wrong Assumptions

C. Reveal Missing / Unnecessary Steps

D. Verify Resource / Asset Availability

E. None of the Above

6. The objective of a _____ is to test the BCP with actual systems without the risk of interrupting the business operation.

A. Fail-Over Test

B. Parallel Test

C. Checklist Test

D. Table-Top Test

E. None of the Above

7. Which choice below is **not** a characteristic or objective that must be considered when conducting Business Continuity Plan (BCP) Table-Top Testing exercises?

A. Simulated Emergency Scenario

B. Test of Decision-Making Process

C. Typically a Two-Day Exercise

D. Mid-Exercise Problem Injections

E. None of the Above

8. The objective of a _____ is to create a full interruption of the business system to definitively test the BCP.

A. Fail-Over Test

B. Parallel Test

C. Checklist Test

D. Table-Top Test

E. None of the Above

9. Which choice below is **not** a potentially suitable event to consider when planning a Business Continuity Plan (BCP) improvisational testing exercises?

A. Scheduled Power Outages

B. Facility Construction Projects

C. Local Government Disaster Drills

D. Minor Structural Floods or Fires

E. None of the Above

10. _____ can create unique opportunities to execute BCP testing scenarios that are relevant to the business operation.

A. Natural Disasters

B. Man-Made Disasters

C. Planned Events

D. Civil Unrest

E. None of the Above

11. Which choice below is **not** an appropriate action to consider when debriefing Business Continuity Plan (BCP) testing and exercise participants?

A. Praise in Public / Criticize in Private

B. Document and Reject Dissenting Opinions

C. Objective Observations Without Judgment

D. Do Not Assign Blame to Participants

E. None of the Above

12. As with all things in the Business Continuity Program, begin setting goals for the testing plan by referring to the _____.

A. Recovery Time Objective

B. Administrative Continuity Plan

C. Business Impact Analysis

D. Business Continuity Manager

E. None of the Above

13. To maximize the benefit to the security department while minimizing management involvement, develop a written testing strategy for the Business Continuity Plan (BCP).

1. True

2. False

14. Business Continuity Plan (BCP) testing can be structured to focus on a plans' strengths and gloss over weaknesses; third-party certification addresses this issue.

1. True

2. False

15. The best Business Continuity Plan (BCP) testing results come from a clear explanation of the feedback of senior leadership and training to show them what to do.

1. True

2. False

16. Whenever an incident occurs that is covered by the Business Continuity Plan (BCP), conduct an after-action review on the next workday after the recovery.

1. True

2. False

17. The objective of Checklist Testing is to create and work through a Business Continuity Plan (BCP) that is unit-specific and understood by senior leadership.

1. True

2. False

18. The objective of a Fail-Over Test is to create a full interruption of the business system to definitively test the Business Continuity Plan (BCP).

1. True

2. False

Creating an Emergency Operations Plan

Disaster Scenario: Chaos

Imagine an organization without a comprehensive BCP/DRP attempting to deal with the aftereffects of a major disaster. Large groups of people are working randomly with no leadership on projects unrelated to actual needs. Without communication, there is no focus on mission-critical priorities and critical actions are overlooked. Repetitious tasks are being initiated and unknowingly undone, and no one at the scene is aware of the project status. In the midst of this chaos the leadership is demanding updates every hour. That is not a good scenario for any organization to experience. Unless leaders can communicate and direct their staff during emergency situations, they are unable to effectively lead, and this scenario might very well become the reality.

Disaster Scenario: Control

Now imagine an organization with a comprehensive BCP/DRP and established procedures for initiating an *Emergency Operations Center* (EOC) attempting to deal with the aftereffects of a major disaster. Everyone knows where to report when the disaster strikes. Teams leaders document the availability of personnel and assign tasks based on their areas of expertise. All recovery actions are directed by a single person prepared to manage the task. Team locations and their composition are noted, relief teams are seamlessly integrated, and the project status board is updated regularly. The EOC allows organizational management to reestablish leadership, allocate resources, and focus on containment and recovery. That would be a better scenario for an organization to face.

The EOC in Limited Emergencies

Disasters can vary in scope and impact. However, an EOC still serves the purpose of a rally point during limited emergencies and short-term, contained disasters. The EOC is typically a place that "everybody knows, and everybody goes," and makes sense for the given situation. It can be a security office with a radio network, or a help desk center with access to the network. No matter what venue is chosen, the EOC should have a contact number everyone would think to call during an emergency. Additionally, the EOC must be preestablished, presupplied, with a location known by everyone before it is needed.

EOC Scope and Purpose

EOC scope and purpose will change from entity to entity based on organizational structure and needs. When it is activated, there are two primary teams: the Containment Team and the Recovery Team. Listed below are five primary functions typically considered by BCP managers when planning the creation of an EOC.

1. Reestablish Organizational Leadership
2. Facilitate the Allocation of Resources
3. Focus on Emergency Containment
4. Initiate the Disaster Recovery Process
5. Minimize Disruption of Management

EOC Characteristics

No two EOC's are identical but most share similar characteristics. Most organizations convert an existing facility with specific capabilities into an EOC as needed. EOC characteristics will change from entity to entity based on organizational structure and needs. Listed below are six primary characteristics typically considered by BCP managers when planning the creation of an EOC.

1. Typically 500 to 2,000 Square Feet
2. Easily Accessible by Road
3. Ready Access for Delivery Services
4. Proximity to Food Service (Dine-In and Take-Out)
5. Proximity to Hotels and Lodging
6. Wired for Data and Communication

EOC Material Requirements

A disaster is not the time to determine what you need in an EOC; careful planning in advance will help ensure faster recovery. EOC material requirements will change from entity to entity based on organizational structure and needs. Listed below are six basic categories of supplies typically considered by BCP managers when planning the material requirements for an EOC.

1. Electricity (Generator and UPS)
2. Emergency Lighting
3. Available Sanitary Facilities
4. Medical Kits and Supplies
5. Pre-Packaged Office Supplies
6. Bottled Water and Non-Perishable Food Items

Unlimited Power Supply (UPS) Considerations

Prior to sizing electrical support units such as generators and UPS, the BCP manager must know what they will need to support in the EOC. This sounds like a common sense statement but in many cases this fact is overlooked. Selection of proper UPS systems will change from entity to entity based on EOC structure and needs. Listed below are five general guidelines typically followed by BCP managers when considering UPS requirements for an EOC.

1. Use a UPS with a Dual-Inverter for Smoother Transition
2. UPS Battery Size: Watts Usage x 1.6 (WPVA)
3. Do Not Use a Generator to Charge the UPS Battery
4. Use a UPS with Logs to Analyze Noise, Sags, and Spikes
5. Establish a Power Shedding Priority Plan for the UPS

EOC Communications

As stated earlier in this domain, unless leaders can communicate and direct their staff during emergency situations, they are unable to effectively lead. The Command Center of the EOC will communicate with teams, news media, vendors, customers, the community, and a broad range of stakeholders. Effective communication is critical to control the organizational message and manage perceptions. Selection of communication systems will change from entity to entity based on organizational structure and EOC needs. Listed below are six basic categories of communication typically considered by BCP managers when planning an EOC.

1. Telephones (Multiple Lines)
2. Radio Communication (Field Crews)
3. Data Communications
4. Organizational Website (Lightweight Pages)
5. Human Messengers (Sensitive Information)
6. Television and AM/FM Radios

EOC Key Personnel

Given the interdisciplinary mission of the EOC, key personnel that represent critical units and functions will be members of the team. Additionally, an important staffing consideration is for every member of the EOC to have a predesignated and cross-trained backup when possible. There will be times when key personnel expected to report to the EOC will be unable to do so.

The more practical reason for cross-trained backup is that key personnel need to rest and refresh themselves. The composition of key personnel will change from entity to entity based on organizational structure and EOC needs. Listed below are six categories of personnel typically considered for the staffing requirements of an EOC.

1. Recovery Site Manager
2. Facility Engineering Manager
3. Public Relations Manager
4. Information Technology Manager
5. Human Resources Manager
6. Security and/or Risk Manager

EOC Command Functions

The EOC has two primary functions during a crisis situation: Command and Control. If the EOC does not take control of the decision-making process, people may tend make expensive and potentially hazardous decisions. The EOC *command functions* will change from entity to entity based on organizational structure and situational needs. Listed below are five EOC command functions typically executed during disasters.

1. **Gather Damage Assessments**: It is important to understand the scope of the disaster and the subsequent impact on the organization prior to initiating any recovery efforts. This can also be problematic as initial information can be incomplete or inaccurate. Gathering assessments that are relevant and accurate will save time and effort during the recovery process.

2. **Develop Action Plans**: Based on the assessments that are gathered and analyzed, an action plan must be developed to contain the damage and recover the critical functions of the organization.

3. **Allocate Resources Efficiently**: Scarce resources must be allocated efficiently to ensure critical functions can be restored quickly. This can be difficult when many requests for resources flow into the EOC simultaneously.

4. **Approve Deviations from the BCP**: Even the best battle plans must be adjusted in the fog of war and the BCP is no exception. Key personnel with a high-level view can allow changes to be made to BCP procedures as required and take the responsibility for justifying those decisions.

5. **Prioritize Responses to Circumstances**: When planned responses lead to unplanned circumstances changes to the pre-planned priorities will inevitably occur. Key personnel in the EOC have the ability to alter response priorities and the authority to ensure the changes are communicated.

EOC Control Functions

The *control function* involves obtaining and dispatching resources based on the direction of the EOC manager. The EOC control functions will change from entity to entity based on organizational structure and situational needs. Listed below are five EOC control functions typically executed during disasters.

1. Ordering Supplies and Services
2. Track Recovery Efforts and Recovery Personnel

3. Implement the Allocated Resources Efficiently
4. Gather Data and Maintain Status Reporting
5. Control the Flow of Information (Internal and External)

Mobile EOC Characteristics

A *mobile EOC* is a viable option for larger organizations with many geographically dispersed facilities. Instead of creating a recovery site for each location a mobile EOC can be dispatched to the area in which the organization was impacted. This tends to be a much more cost-effective solution than multiple recovery sites. Vehicles used as an EOC tend to be large—such as a recreational vehicle or camping trailer—and are equipped to provide comfort for extended lengths of time.

This vehicle is preloaded with everything necessary to establish an EOC, including a generator and tent for expanding the work area. The mobile EOC configuration will change from entity to entity based on organizational structure and geographical needs. Listed below are five characteristics typically associated with mobile EOC's regardless of their size, make, or model.

1. Pre-Supplied with Generators and Tents
2. Requires Cellular Capability for Voice and Data
3. Digitized Floor Plans with Wiring Drawings
4. Door Keys for Critical Access Points
5. Security Credentials for Mobile Response Staff

DOMAIN 06

Creating an Emergency Operations Plan

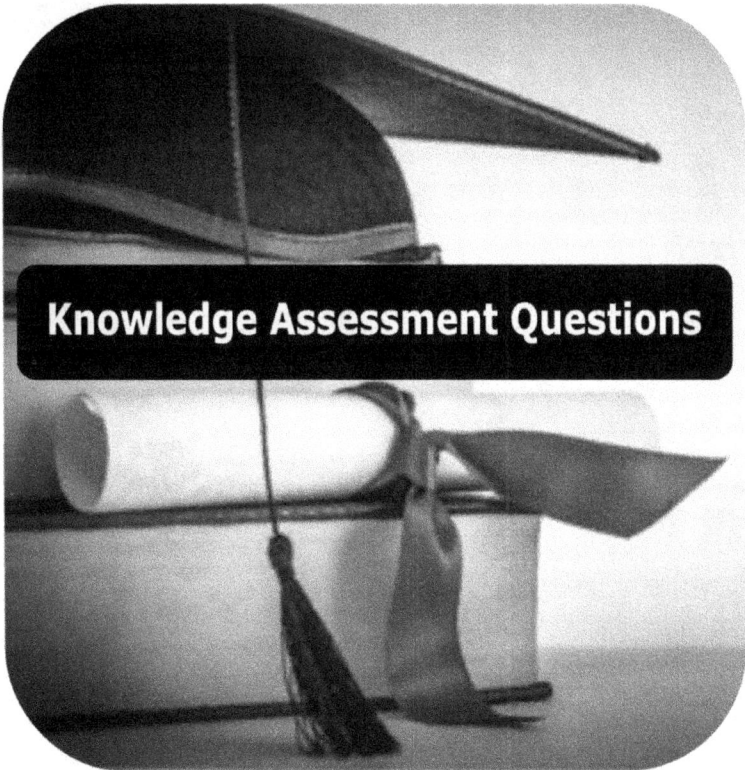

Knowledge Assessment Questions

The following knowledge assessment questions are presented as true / false, multiple choice, and fill-in-the-blank. The correct answers are provided in an Answer Key at the end of the text. These questions may or may not be presented on the actual certification exam.

Domain 06: Knowledge Assessment Questions

1. Which choice below is **not** a characteristic of a poorly planned response to a disaster without the use of a Business Continuity Plan (BCP)?

A. Large Groups Working Randomly

B. Action Directed by Single Person

C. Unaware of Status of Progress

D. No Coordinated Mission-Critical Action

E. None of the Above

2. When an Emergency Operations Center is activated two primary teams are deployed: the _____ Team and the Recovery Team.

A. Incident Response

B. Containment

C. Disaster

D. Mobile

E. None of the Above

3. Which choice below is a characteristic or consideration for a temporary Emergency Operations Center (EOC)?

A. Rally Point for Limited Emergencies

B. Short-Term Contained Disasters

C. "Everybody Knows, Everybody Goes"

D. Number People Would Think to Call

E. All of the Above

4. An important command function an EOC will undertake will be to _____ when first activated to take control of the decision-making process.

A. Order Supplies and Services

B. Track Recovery Effort / Personnel

C. Implement Allocated Resources

D. Gather Damage Assessments

E. None of the Above

5. Which choice below is **not** a condition to be considered when discussing the characteristics of an Emergency Operations Center (EOC)?

A. Easily Accessible by Airport

B. Ready Access for Delivery Services

C. Wired for Data and Communication

D. Proximity to Hotels / Lodging

E. All of the Above

6. An important control function an EOC will undertake will be to _____ when first activated to take control of the decision-making process.

A. Develop Action Plans

B. Prioritize Responses to Circumstances

C. Control the Flow of Information

D. Approve Deviations from the BCP

E. None of the Above

7. Which choice below is **not** an item or action to be considered when planning the Uninterruptible Power Supply (UPS) needs of an Emergency Operations Center (EOC)?

A. Dual-Inverter for Smoother Transition

B. Establish a Power Shedding Priority Plan

C. Use Generator to Recharge UPS

D. Logs to Analyze Noise, Sags, and Spikes

E. All of the Above

8. Prior to _____ electrical support units such as generators and UPS, you must know what they will need to support in the EOC.

A. Sizing

B. Purchasing

C. Deploying

D. Approving

E. All of the Above

9. Which choice below is **not** a factor to be considered when planning for the key personnel needs of an Emergency Operations Center (EOC)?

A. Recovery Site Manager

B. Human Resources Manager

C. Information Technology Manager

D. Payroll / Finance Manager

E. All of the Above

10. Most organizations _____ an existing facility with specific capabilities into an Emergency Operations Center as needed.

A. Convert

B. Locate

C. Purchase

D. Lease

E. All of the Above

11. Which choice below is **not** a benefit or characteristic to be considered when planning for the use of a Mobile Emergency Operations Center (MEOC)?

A. More Cost Effective Than Multiple EOC's

B. Pre-Supplied with Generator / Tents

C. Does Not Require Cellular for Voice / Data

D. Security Credentials for Mobile Staff

E. All of the Above

12. A disaster is not the time to determine what you need in an Emergency Operations Center; _____ will help ensure a faster recovery.

A. Backup Media

B. Information Technology

C. Adequate Budgets

D. Careful Planning

E. None of the Above

13. An Emergency Operations Center (EOC) allows organizational management to reassign leadership, locate resources, and focus on daily business operations.

1. True

2. False

14. The Emergency Operations Center (EOC) control function involves obtaining and dispatching resources based on the direction of the EOC manager.

1. True

2. False

15. When an Emergency Operations Center (EOC) is activated, there are two primary teams: the Management Team and the Support Team.

1. True

2. False

16. An important staffing consideration is for every member of the Emergency Operations Center (EOC) to have a predesignated and cross-trained backup when possible.

1. True

2. False

17. A disaster is the perfect time to determine what you need in an Emergency Operations Center (EOC); observed needs will help ensure faster recovery.

1. True

2. False

18. The Command Center will communicate with teams, news media, vendors, customers, the community, and a broad range of stakeholders.

1. True

2. False

DOMAIN 07

Recovery Site
Management and Workflows

Recovery Site Key Definitions

Cold Site:

A cold site is a business location that is used for backup in the event of a disruptive operational disaster at the normal business site and typically does not have the necessary equipment to resume prompt operations.

Warm Site:

A warm site is a business location that is used for backup in the event of a disruptive operational disaster at the normal business site and is typically suited for bringing up non-essential systems that don't require the immediate restoration that mission-critical systems do.

Hot Site:

A hot site is a business location that is used for backup in the event of a disruptive operational disaster at the normal business site and is typically a fully operational commercial disaster recovery service that allows continuity of operations in a very short period.

Reciprocal Site:

A reciprocal site is a business location shared by multiple organizations that is used for backup in the event of a disruptive operational disaster at the normal business site and is typically suited for similarly configured organizations with similar recovery requirements.

Assembly Point Considerations

A conditioned response is critical to effective crisis management; time for recovery is decreased when teams can be assembled and tasked quickly. This capability requires the selection of a predetermined assembly point all personnel involved in either the containment or recovery mission. *Assembly point considerations* scenarios will change from entity to entity based on organizational structure and needs. Listed below are seven factors typically considered by BCP managers that can influence potential locations.

1. Location During Work Hours
2. Location Outside of Work Hours
3. Access to Data and Telephone Services
4. Access to Wireless and Internet Services
5. Well Lit at all Hours
6. Easy for Personnel to Locate
7. Ample Parking Away from Main Entrance

Recovery Site Manager

The *Recovery Site Manager* represents the senior leadership and must be able to manage technical and non-technical activities. The individual must also have the authority to make critical decisions without the need of leadership approval. The requirements and selection criteria will change from entity to entity based on organizational structure and needs. Listed below are five primary responsibilities typically assigned to the Recovery Site Manager.

1. Assigns Tasks to all Personnel
2. Oversees the Tracking of Personnel
3. Maintains the Recovery Activity Log
4. Validates Successful Recoveries
5. Directs Status Reporting (Incoming and Outgoing)

Assign Personnel Tasks

When a recovery site is activated following a disaster there is no time to argue about job boundaries or authority. Site personnel must do what they are instructed to do, when they are instructed to do it, even when the tasks fall outside their job description. It is common for IT personnel to push-back when assigned non-technical jobs such as sanitation or food delivery. Although the range of tasks and assignments is broad and far-reaching there are five primary categories of tasks the Recovery Site Manager must consider.

1. Assign and Ensure Site Security
2. Appoint an Alternate (Backup) Site Manager
3. Assign Status Reporting Duties
4. Assign Shifts and Publish a Rest Plan
5. Reassign Employees as Required

Site Personnel Tracking

Knowing who is on-site ensures safety and efficiency of recovery site staff and provides documentation acknowledgement after a successful recovery. If a smart card access system is operational at the site, the logs will be generated electronically. If not, a roster kept by security personnel at the site entrance can be used. The means and methods of personnel tracking will change from entity to entity based on organizational structure and needs. Listed below are five typical objectives associated with personnel tracking.

1. Facilitates Employee Assignments
2. Helps Avoid Wasting Time
3. Identify the Need for Rest Periods
4. Account for Missing or Overdue Staff
5. Logs are Useful for Post-Recovery Actions

Recovery Activity Log

The *recovery site activity log* is used to record critical events during the recovery and helps with post-recovery analysis and planning. It is usually maintained by one individual assigned by the Recovery Site Manager. The policies and procedures associated with this log will change from entity to entity based on organizational structure and needs. Listed below are five typical categories of information tracked by the activity log.

1. Mandatory Task Initiation Reporting
2. Mandatory Task Completion Reporting
3. Requests for Service and Supplies
4. Status Reports to and from the Command Center
5. A Source of Information for Gantt Charts

Recovery Gantt Chart Function

The *recovery site Gantt chart* is publicly posted, easy to read, and answers the question, "*When will it be ready?*" It is usually used for hour-by-hour status reporting and serves to identify progress delays in advance. The timeframes and formats of Gantt charts will change from entity to entity based on organizational structure and needs. Listed below are five typical characteristics associated with a Gantt chart and its use.

1. Tracks Hour-by-Hour Recovery Status
2. Creates a Logical Sequence of IT Recovery
3. The Chart is Created During BCP Testing
4. The Chart Compares Estimated and Actual Times
5. Identify Recovery Delays and Predicts Completion Times

Validate Successful Recoveries

Validating successful recoveries provides a layered testing strategy that is useful for catching errors and reducing the time and need to troubleshoot issues repeatedly. Locating the specific technician originally responsible for recovering the system in question—who may already be involved in another recovery effort—can prove to be troublesome. The process by which successful recoveries are validated will change from entity to entity based on organizational structure and needs. Listed below are the five typical phases associated with validating recoveries.

1. The Application and/or System is Restored
2. It is Tested by the Initial Technician
3. The Functionality is Tested by a "Power User"
4. The Recovered System is Released for General Use
5. The Command Center is Notified of the Success

Recovery Site Work Area Considerations

Designing the *recovery site work area* is a team effort that requires critical departments to be involved in every step of the process. It involves much more than the placement of desks, chairs, and filing cabinets. The BCP manager must also take into consideration such as building codes and occupancy limits that remain in effect even during disasters. The process for planning work areas will change from entity to entity based on organizational structure and needs. Listed below are the four typical characteristics to consider when planning a recovery site work area.

1. Plan for 70 to 80 Square Feet per Person
2. The Square Footage Accounts for All Building Space
3. Design Work Areas to be 36" W x 24" D
4. Rotate Shifts to Maximize Work Area Space

Team Member Seating

Team member seating is a critical consideration when planning the recovery site work area that prevents "first come, sit anywhere" chaos. People tend to be conscious of seating arrangements, and even more so when confidential communication is required. The process for planning team member seating will change from entity to entity based on the physical work area and organizational needs. Listed below are five guidelines typically considered by the BCP manager when planning team member seating arrangements.

1. Collocate Interactive Teams (i.e., Finance and Payroll)
2. Recognize that Human Resources and Legal Need Privacy
3. Label Every Desk by Department
4. Label Every Cabinet by Content
5. Suspend Location Signs Conspicuously from the Ceiling

Direct Status Reporting

One individual (and a backup) will be directed to be responsible for maintaining all status reporting between the disaster location and the recovery site. Structured and effective communication is a two-way street that is critical to reduce the chaos and confusion caused by stressful environments. The timeframes and format of status reports will change from entity to entity based on the direction of the Recovery Site Manager and organizational needs. Listed below are five areas of communication typically included in all status reporting initiatives.

1. Status of the Restoration Timeline
2. Names of Personnel at the Recovery Site
3. Supplies and/or Services Required by Recovery Site
4. Progress Updates from the Disaster Location
5. Status of Ongoing Recovery Site Requests

Backup Tape Transport Considerations

Although organizations are trending in the direction of moving backup data from magnetic media to a cloud solution, many legacy systems still rely on tape for data backup. Long-term storage using a professional service does not usually raise concerns, but the transport of magnetic backup media to the recovery site presents specialized and high-risk challenges for the BCP manager. The tape storage and transportation methods will change from entity to entity based on organizational technology and needs. Listed below are five areas of concern the BCP manager should consider when planning the transport of magnetic media to a recovery site.

1. Magnetic Tape is Degraded by Temperature Change
2. Tape can be Damaged by Sunlight and/or Air Particles
3. Always Handle Magnetic Tape with Lint-Free Gloves
4. Tape can be Damaged by Electronics and/or Machinery
5. Tape can Become Outdated (and Useless) Quickly

Data Deduplication

Deduplication of data provides an efficient compression, single instance storage solution that reduces required storage space and recovery time. Source-based deduplication occurs before backup, allows for less storage space, but may create bottlenecks in slower systems. Target-based deduplication occurs at the backup facility, tends to be much faster, but requires a larger amount of storage space which may be underutilized.

Digital Communication Considerations

When planning for specialized issues associated with the restoration of digital communication, the BCP manager must document alternative communication methods in the event planned methods prove to be ineffective. Communication strategies and priorities will change from entity to entity based on organizational technology and needs. Listed below are five areas of concern typically considered by BCP managers when developing contingency plans for digital communication needs.

1. Note the Location of Wiring Closets and Patch Panels
2. Ensure Route Separation for 100% Redundancy
3. Map Internal and External Cabling Routes
4. Conduct an Inventory of Communication Assets
5. Identify Communication Restoration Priorities

"Call-Tree" Challenges

Despite advances in communications technology, there are a few organizations that still employee the "call-tree" methodology for mass internal notifications. Given current alternatives, this method for team member notification is prone to error and an inefficient option at larger scales. "Call-Trees" are better than nothing, but not by much.

Mass communication strategies and methodologies will change from entity to entity based on organizational policy and needs. Listed below are six areas concern a BCP manager should take into consideration when contemplating the use of this method for mass notification during disasters.

1. People on the List may be Difficult to Reach
2. The Person may Neglect to Call Others on the List
3. Some People do not Respond to Unknown Numbers
4. Some People Turn Off Work Phones After Hours
5. Cellular Networks can Become Overloaded in Disasters
6. Curiosity and Conversations Slow Down the Processes

SMS Notification System

Short Message Service (SMS) notifications are an efficient mass communication method that allow the same message to be broadcast via text to everyone at the same time. This method is much more efficient than the "call-tree" system for mass internal notification. SMS strategies and implementations will change from entity to entity based on organizational technology and needs. Listed below are five general benefits the BCP manager should consider when planning the use of SMS for notification strategies.

1. Virtually Every Mobile Device can Receive Text
2. Text Messages are Read More Quickly
3. SMS Utilizes Little Amounts of Bandwidth on Networks
4. SMS Works if Data Network is Overloaded
5. SMS does not Require the Internet to Function

SMS Notification Methodology

Although internal recipients of mass notifications can receive a text message at the same time, various levels of management and team members with distinct roles will not need to hear the same messages. The verbiage of messages sent to various personnel will change from entity to entity based on organizational policy and a listing of multiple tiered contacts in the SMS system. Listed below are the four tiers of organizational personnel a BCP manager should consider when developing an SMS notification strategy.

1. Executives and Senior Management
2. Functional and Unit Management
3. Line Managers and Supervisors
4. "All-Call" General Notification to Organizational Personnel

DOMAIN 07

Recovery Site
Management and Workflows

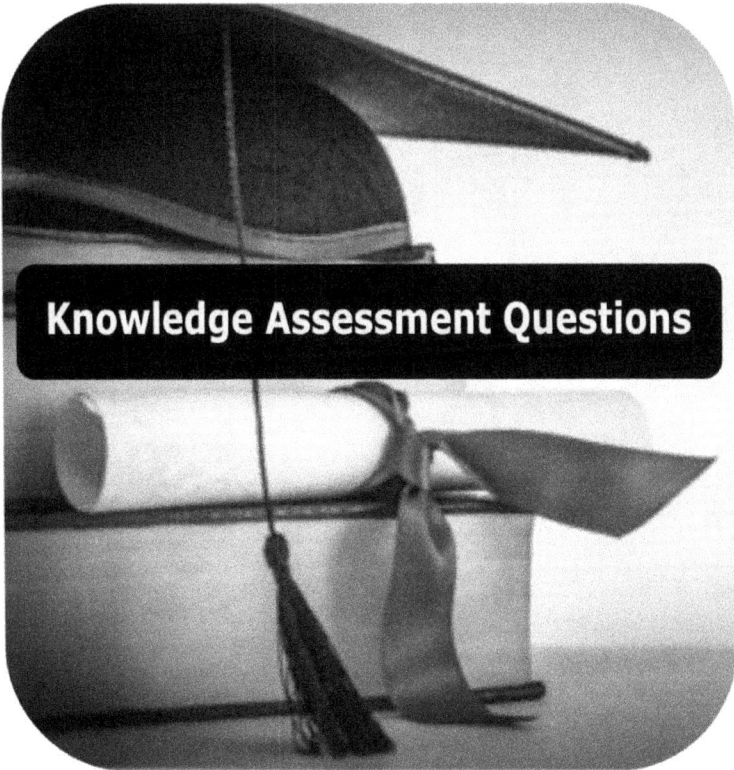

Knowledge Assessment Questions

The following knowledge assessment questions are presented as true / false, multiple choice, and fill-in-the-blank. The correct answers are provided in an Answer Key at the end of the text. These questions may or may not be presented on the actual certification exam.

Domain 07: Knowledge Assessment Questions

1. "*A business location that is used for backup in the event of a disruptive operational disaster at the normal business site and typically does not have the necessary equipment to resume prompt operations.*"

A. Hot Site

B. Reciprocal Site

C. Cold Site

D. Warm Site

E. None of the Above

2. The _____ represents the senior leadership and must be able to manage technical and non-technical activities.

A. Business Continuity Manager

B. Information Security Manager

C. Recovery Site Manager

D. Human Resource Manager

E. None of the Above

3. "*A business location that is used for backup in the event of a disruptive operational disaster at the normal business site and is typically a fully-operational commercial disaster recovery service that allows continuity of operations in a very short period.*"

A. Hot Site

B. Reciprocal Site

C. Cold Site

D. Warm Site

E. None of the Above

4. When a recovery site is activated following a disaster there is no time to argue about job boundaries or _____.

A. Assignments

B. Payroll

C. Achievements

D. Authority

E. None of the Above

5. Which choice below is **not** an appropriate consideration when discussing potential locations for a personnel assembly point?

A. Well Lit at All Hours

B. Ample Parking Away from Entrance

C. Secure and Confidential Location

D. During Work Hours / After Work Hours

E. None of the Above

6. The recovery site activity log is used to record significant events during the recovery and helps with post-recovery analysis and _____.

A. Reporting

B. Planning

C. Financing

D. Communication

E. None of the Above

7. Which choice below is **not** a responsibility of the Recovery Site Manager when assigning tasks to staff?

A. Assign and Ensure Site Security

B. Assign Shifts and Publish Rest Plan

C. Assign Status Reporting Duties

D. Assign Disaster Site Responsibilities

E. None of the Above

8. Validating successful recoveries provides a(n) _____ testing strategy that is useful for catching errors and reducing the need to troubleshoot.

A. Layered

B. Linear

C. Continuous

D. Documented

E. None of the Above

9. Which choice below is **not** a purpose of a Recovery Activity Log located at a disaster recovery site?

A. Efficient Substitute for Gantt Chart

B. Mandatory Task Initiation Reporting

C. Status Reports to Command Center

D. Requests for Service and Supplies

E. None of the Above

10. Designing the recovery site layout is a team effort that requires _____ to be involved in the process.

A. Specialized Staff

B. Senior Management

C. External Stakeholders

D. Critical Departments

E. None of the Above

11. Which choice below is **not** a consideration when planning for the use of magnetic back-up media to be transported to the recovery site?

A. Degraded by Temperature Change

B. Damaged by Sunlight / Air Particles

C. Damaged by Electronics / Machinery

D. Can Become Outdated Quickly

E. None of the Above

12. The _____ method for team member notification is prone to error and an inefficient option at larger scales.

A. Text Message

B. MMS

C. Call Tree

D. Facebook Chat

E. None of the Above

13. A conditioned response is critical to effective crisis management; time for recovery is decreased when teams can be tasked quickly.

1. True

2. False

14. Different levels of management and team members with different roles will need to hear the same broadcast messages to ensure everyone is informed.

1. True

2. False

15. When a recovery site is activated following a disaster, there is no time to argue about job boundaries or authority.

1. True

2. False

16. The "call tree" method for team member notification is prone to error and only an efficient option for larger organizations.

1. True

2. False

17. The recovery site activity log is used to record significant events during the recovery and helps with post-recovery analysis and planning.

1. True

2. False

18. Duplication of data provides an efficient compression, single instance storage solution that reduces required storage space and recovery time.

1. True

2. False

DOMAIN 08

Preparing for
Epidemics and Pandemics

Epidemic and Pandemic Key Definitions

Epidemic:

A widespread occurrence of a disease in a community that spreads quickly and affects many individuals at the same time.

Pandemic:

An epidemic that becomes very widespread and affects a whole region, a continent, or the world due to a susceptible population and causes a high degree of mortality.

Seasonal Flu vs. Pandemic Flu

Seasonal Influenza	Pandemic Influenza
Predictable Patterns	Unpredictable Patterns
Occurs Annually	Occurs Rarely
Some Immunity Exists	No Preexisting Immunity
Vaccines Initially Available	No Vaccines Initially Available
Healthy Patients Lower Risk	Healthy Patients High Risk
Modest Impact on Society	Major Impact on Society

6 Phases of a Pandemic

The *World Health Organization* (WHO) has divided pandemics into six phases; the phase will dictate when a disaster is declared. The phase at which point a disaster declaration is made will change from entity to entity based on organizational structure and needs. Listed below are the six phases of a pandemic.

1. Animal to Animal
2. Animal to Human

3. Human to Human (Limited)
4. Human to Human (Community)
5. Country to Country (Region)
6. Country to Country (Global)

Flu Epidemics: Facts and Statistics

Despite the distinction of definitions between epidemics and pandemics, an epidemic is simply a localized pandemic. Impacts of seasonal influenza on an organization can be severe. Listed below are six epidemic statistics for the BCP manager to consider when creating the Epidemic / Pandemic BCP. The statistics have been assembled by the *Centers for Disease Control and Prevention* and represent 2019-2020 averages (https://www.cdc.gov/flu).

1. Flu is a Contagious Respiratory Illness
2. Flu is a Virus-Based Infection (not Bacteria)
3. Flu is Most Contagious in the First 3-4 Days
4. Infection Vectors: Eyes, Nose and Mouth
5. Infection Radius: Up to 6 Feet
6. There are 9.3 – 49 Million Flu Illnesses per Year

Flu Epidemics: Vulnerable Populations

When an Epidemic / Pandemic BCP is written it is important not to forget the family members of organizational staff. In addition to the possibility they may be a member of a vulnerable population, a family members' illness can keep healthy staff away from their organization. Listed below are six characteristics of vulnerable populations during influenza epidemics. The statistics have been assembled by the *Centers for Disease Control and Prevention* and represent 2019-2020 averages (https://www.cdc.gov/flu).

1. Children Younger than Age 5
2. Adults Older than Age 65
3. Pregnant Women (Up to 2-Weeks Postpartum)
4. People with Weakened Immune Systems
5. People with Chronic Illnesses
6. People with a Body Mass Index ≥ 40

Impacts of Flu on Organizations

The direct, indirect, and delayed impacts of a flu epidemic on an organization can be significant in both human and financial terms. The six statistics below have been assembled by the company *Challenger, Gray and Christmas, Inc.* and represent 2019-2020 averages (https://www.challengergray.com).

1. 900,000 People Hospitalized and 80,000 People Dead
2. $10.4 Billion in Direct Medical Expenses
3. $15.3 Billion in Lost Revenue
4. $21 Billion in Lost Productivity
5. 17 Million Total Workdays Missed
6. $856 per Individual in Lost Wages (25 Million Workers)

Employee Flu Vaccinations

Providing flu vaccinations to organizational staff has proven to significantly lower the impacts experienced by the organization and the spread of the disease between staff. However, no one can be compelled to submit to a mandatory vaccination. The availability of immunization plans for staff will change from entity to entity based on organizational policy and employee need. The five statistics below representing 2019-2020 averages have been assembled by the organization *Healthline* and should be considered by BCP managers incorporating a vaccination plan into their Epidemic / Pandemic BCP (https://www.healthline.com).

1. Delivered by Injection or Nasal Spray
2. Average Cost to Organization is $0 - $25 per Individual
3. Vaccinations Prevented 5.3 Million Illnesses
4. Vaccinations Prevented 2.6 Million Medical Visits
5. Vaccinations Prevented 85,000 Hospitalizations

The Epidemic / Pandemic BCP Team

Unique events such as epidemics and pandemics require unique solutions to mitigate risks and reduce potential impacts. Just as the Epidemic / Pandemic BCP is unlike any other component of the entire organizational BCP, the team chosen to manage this plan must be unique as well. The team composition will change from entity to entity based on organizational structure and need, but BCP managers should attempt to include internal or external team members with medical training whenever possible. Listed below are five departments from which BCP team members should be selected, as these departments will have a significant impact before, during, and after an epidemic or pandemic.

1. Human Resource Management
2. Information Technology Management
3. Facilities Management
4. Logistics Management
5. Sales and Operations Management

The Epidemic / Pandemic Risk Assessment

The risk assessment for an epidemic or pandemic is based on a fluctuating business impact analysis and will vary based on the organizational unit responsibility and mission. The business impact analysis and subsequent risk assessment will change from entity to entity based on organizational structure and need. Listed below are six areas of consideration for the BCP manager conducting this type of assessment.

1. Employee-to-Employee Contact (Internal)
2. Employee-to-Customer Contact (External Sales)
3. Contact with Infected Items (Rent and Return)
4. Contact from Travel (Sales and Operations)
5. Impact on Raw Materials and Supplies (Upstream)
6. Impact on Customer Demand (Downstream)

Human Resource Management

Human Resource and Information Technology Management each have responsibilities that provide them with unique roles during the execution of an epidemic or pandemic BCP strategy. They are both in a position to recognize the organizational policies that are most likely to be impacted by such an event, and they are both in a position to implement risk mitigation solutions to lessen impact.

In short, Human Resource Management can create the flexibility in employee policies required to minimize impact on the operation, and Information Technology Management can create the distance between staff required to minimize the spread of the influenza. The extent to which organizational policies can be modified will change from entity to entity based on organizational structure and need. Listed below are six policy areas the BCP manager should consider when developing the Epidemic / Pandemic BCP.

1. Review and Modify the Virtual Worker Policy
2. Review and Modify the Attendance Policy
3. Identify Trained Substitutes for Key Personnel
4. Review and Modify the Company Travel Policy
5. Consider Rotating, Alternate, and Flexible Shifts
6. Consider a Free Immunization Policy (Voluntary)

Remote Worker Security Risks

The best way to prevent the spread of any disease is by creating distance between people. An organization can accomplish this in many ways, but the implementation of a remote worker policy is the most common solution. If a BCP manager is creating a plan for an organization with a limited remote capability, they must understand the risks associated with allowing staff this capability if they have not had it previously. Listed below are statistics from a *Cisco/InsightExpress* (https://www.cisco.com) survey of staff using organizational laptops while away from the office.

1. 40% Admitted to Online Shopping
2. 21% Admitted to Sharing Their Device
3. 10% Admitted to Risky Wireless Behavior
4. 50% Admitted to Using Personal Devices on the Network
5. 38% Admitted to Opening ALL Email Attachments
6. 4% Admitted to Loss or Theft of a Company Device

The Epidemic and Pandemic Communication Plan

An effective communication plan allows an organization to provide accurate information to staff well in advance of the disaster and test current mass communication methods to ensure that contact information is correct. Listed below are six common communication methods the BCP manager should consider when developing the epidemic / pandemic communication plan.

1. Posters and Flyers
2. Team Meetings
3. SMS Notifications
4. The Organizations' Website
5. Toll-Free Hotlines
6. CDC Instructional Videos (Posted on the Website)

Common Area Sanitation Plan

Common area sanitation plans help to reduce the spread of disease and bring precautionary awareness to the forefront of peoples' minds. These tasks must be assigned; do not expect people to volunteer. Listed below are six common areas and fixtures the BCP manager should consider when developing the sanitation plan.

1. Doorknobs and Push Plates
2. Banister Rails
3. Light Switches
4. Lunchroom, Breakroom, and Meeting Areas
5. Vending Machines
6. Shared Workstations and Equipment

Post-Epidemic and Pandemic Considerations

The scope of post-incident actions will change from entity to entity based on the extent of the impact to the organizational structure. BCP managers must maintain vigilance as epidemic/pandemic cases decline and utilize continuous communication until the event is officially declared over. Listed below are six actions the BCP manager should consider when the crisis has officially passed.

1. Make an Official Announcement that the BCP is Closed
2. Review the Effectiveness of the Plan
3. Identify the Impact on Employees and Families
4. Identify the Impact on Sales, Services, and Products
5. Identify the Impact on Suppliers, Customers, and Logistics
6. Provide Formal Recognition for People Involved

DOMAIN 08

Preparing for Epidemics and Pandemics

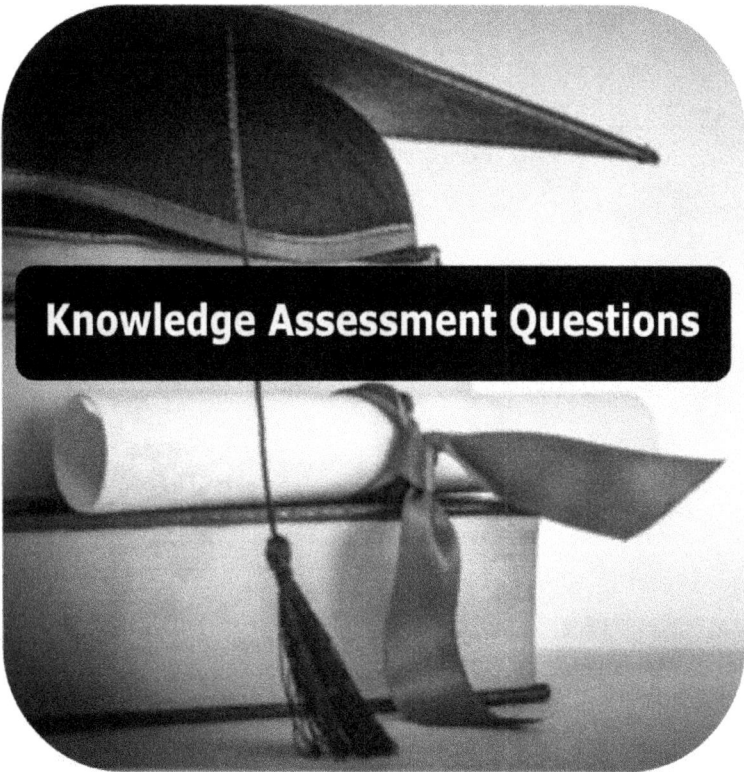

Knowledge Assessment Questions

The following knowledge assessment questions are presented as true / false, multiple choice, and fill-in-the-blank. The correct answers are provided in an Answer Key at the end of the text. These questions may or may not be presented on the actual certification exam.

Domain 08: Knowledge Assessment Questions

1. Which choice below does **not** qualify as a phase of a pandemic as defined by the World Health Organization (WHO)?

A. Animal to Human (Initial)

B. Human to Animal (Limited)

C. Human to Human (Community)

D. Country to Country (Regional)

E. None of the Above

2. Seasonal influenza has the distinctive characteristic of _____ that distinguishes it from pandemic influenza counterpart.

A. Occurs Rarely

B. Major Impact on Society

C. Unpredictable Patterns

D. Some Immunity Exists

E. None of the Above

3. Which choice below is **not** a valid consideration for Senior Leadership when planning for post-epidemic or post-pandemic actions and operations?

A. Impact on Employees and Families

B. Impact on Sales, Services, and Products

C. Impact on Suppliers / Logistics

D. Recognition for People Involved

E. All of the Above

4. Pandemic influenza has the distinctive characteristic of _____ that distinguishes it from epidemic influence counterpart.

A. No Preexisting Immunity

B. Healthy Patients Have Lower Risk

C. Unpredictable Patterns

D. Vaccines Initially Available

E. None of the Above

5. Which choice below is **not** a valid fact or statistic regarding influenza epidemics?

A. Contagious Respiratory Illness

B. Virus-Based Infection (not Bacteria)

C. Infection Radius: Up to 12 Feet

D. 9.3 – 49 Million Illnesses per Year

E. None of the Above

6. Epidemics and Pandemics require unique solutions and unique BCP teams that should include members with _____.

A. Good Work History

B. Medical Experience

C. Time and Availability

D. Marketing Experience

E. None of the Above

7. Which choice below is **not** a valid consideration for Human Resource Management when planning for influenza epidemics or pandemics?

A. Review Virtual Worker Policy

B. Mandatory Immunization Policy

C. Review Alternate and Flexible Shifts

D. Review Company Travel Policy

E. None of the Above

8. The Epidemic / Pandemic BCP is based on a(n) _____ Business Impact Analysis and will vary based on unit responsibility.

A. Fluctuating

B. Documented

C. Approved

D. Certified

E. None of the Above

9. Which choice below is **not** a valid fact or statistic regarding vulnerable populations impacted by influenza epidemics?

A. Children Younger than Age 5

B. Pregnant Women (2-Weeks Postpartum)

C. People with Chronic Illnesses

D. People with Body Mass Index ≥ 20

E. None of the Above

10. Human Resources and IT are the core of the Epidemic / Pandemic BCP and can identify _____ impacted by risk mitigation efforts.

A. External Stakeholders

B. Operational Data

C. Temporary Employees

D. Company Policies

E. None of the Above

11. Which choice below is **not** a valid concern when conducting an Epidemic / Pandemic Risk Assessment?

A. Employee-to-Employee Contact

B. Employee-to-Customer Contact

C. Cost of International Travel

D. Contact with Infected Items

E. None of the Above

12. The _____ phase of a Pandemic as defined by the WHO is typically the phase at which an Epidemic / Pandemic BCP is initiated.

A. Human to Human (limited)

B. Human to Human (community)

C. Country to Country (region)

D. Country to Country (global)

E. None of the Above

13. The World Health Organization has divided pandemics into seven phases; the last phase will dictate when a disaster is declared.

1. True

2. False

14. Maintain vigilance as epidemic / pandemic cases decline and utilize continuous communication until the event is officially declared over.

1. True

2. False

15. When writing a Pandemic Plan into the Business Continuity Plan (BCP), it is important to consider the personal possessions of organizational staff.

1. True

2. False

16. Human Resources and IT are the core of the Epidemic / Pandemic Business Continuity Plan (BCP) and can identify company policies impacted by risk mitigation efforts.

1. True

2. False

17. The Epidemic / Pandemic Risk Assessment is based on a predicted Business Impact Analysis (BIA) and will vary based on those writing the assessment.

1. True

2. False

18. Despite the distinction of definitions between epidemics and pandemics, an epidemic is simply a localized pandemic.

1. True

2. False

The Role of Cloud Computing in Disaster Planning

Definition of Cloud Computing

NIST SP 800-145:

Cloud computing is a model for enabling ubiquitous, convenient, on-demand network access to a shared pool of configurable computing resources (e.g., networks, servers, storage, applications, and services) that can be rapidly provisioned and released with minimal management effort or service provider interaction. This cloud model is composed of five essential characteristics, three service models, and four deployment models.

Cloud Computing Characteristics

Despite many functions and configurations, five characteristics are accepted as part of the cloud computing definition.

1. On-Demand Self-Service
2. Broad Network Access
3. Resource Pooling
4. Rapid Elasticity
5. Measured Service (Metering)

Defining the Existing Operational State

Although cloud platforms are gaining in popularity as solutions for BCP/DRP managers, not every organization needs to migrate their data. The purpose of identifying the organizations' existing operational state is to determine its needs, not the solutions for those needs. Analysis and assessment methods will change from entity to entity based on organizational structure and needs. Listed below are seven actions typically taken by BCP managers when defining the existing operational state of an organization.

1. Interview Senior Leadership
2. Interview Unit Managers
3. Interview Internal End Users of Systems

4. Interview External Customers
5. Collect and Analyze Marketing Data
6. Collect and Analyze Network Traffic
7. Identify Regulatory and Compliance Requirements

Reducing Infrastructure Expenses

Migrating data to the cloud as part of the BCP can be an attractive option for many organizations. Technical resources tend to be either underutilized which wastes money, or overutilized to the point of potential failure. Cloud platforms minimize this concern by providing metered services—"pay as you go"—that allow clients to only pay for the services they need. The cloud can also serve as a backup during peak periods to support existing internal legacy systems, a term referred to as "cloud bursting."

Reducing Personnel and Payroll Expenses

Organizations may also take advantage of cloud services to reduce personnel and payroll expenses associated with IT functions. Managing data and its required infrastructure is neither a core function of most organizations, nor is it a profit center for the business process itself. Managing data requires specialized skills. It is difficult to recruit and retain qualified IT personnel and they tend to be disproportionately more expensive than non-technical staff. Cloud platforms minimize this concern by reducing the number of data management staff needed by the organization and including the costs of data management as part of the contract.

Sharing Regulatory and Compliance Costs

Even in a cloud environment, the BCP manager must be aware that organizations cannot transfer the risk or liability associated with disclosure of *Personally Identifiable Information* (PII). However, the cloud is structured that regulatory compliance packages can be included when required by specific industries and applied to the customer account. These packages are negotiated into the service contract and remove the organizations' need to manage individual controls, reducing both organizational expenses and effort.

Cloud Computing Service Models

Cloud services are typically offered in three standard models based on provider capability and customer needs. The types of models selected will change from entity to entity based on organizational structure and BCP goals. Listed below are the three standard cloud models and a few examples of their corresponding functions.

1. **IaaS** (Infrastructure as a Service): In this model, the provider is responsible for providing the hardware and the infrastructure to manage their data needs.

2. **PaaS** (Platform as a Service): In this model, the provider is responsible for providing IaaS capabilities, but also provides the client with numerous varieties of operating systems as needed.

3. **SaaS** (Software as a Service): In the model, the provider is responsible for providing IaaS and PaaS capabilities, but also provides the client with applications such as CRM and email as needed.

Infrastructure as a Service (IaaS)

In the IaaS model, the cloud service provider contracts access to its infrastructure and is fully responsible for its administration. This model is typically utilized for clients with limited needs, such as archiving data for BCP/DRP purposes. Utilization of this model will change from entity to entity based on organizational structure and needs. The cloud customer provides the operating systems, required applications, and is responsible for the maintenance of both. This tends to increase security for the clients' data, as the party controlling the O/S controls security.

Platform as a Service (PaaS)

In the PaaS model, the cloud service provider offers not only the IaaS capability but provides the customer with operating systems as well. The provider can offer clients multiple operating systems simultaneously which can be useful for software development that must be tested in isolated (non-production) environments. Utilization of this model will change from entity to entity based on organizational structure and software development needs. These operating systems are typically hardened, maintained by the provider, and allow developers to conduct compatibility testing for their software with multiple O/S's.

Software as a Service (SaaS)

In the SaaS model, the customer receives all the underlying IaaS and PaaS capabilities, as well as end user applications that are needed by the organization. The cloud provider is responsible for the administration of the infrastructure, operating systems, and all applications. This is a hosted full production environment in which the client is only required to upload and utilize data. Utilization of this model will change from entity to entity based on organizational structure and the applications required for daily operations. Listed below are a few typical uses of the SaaS model.

1. Google Docs, MS Office 365
2. CRM Software
3. Accounting Software

Public Cloud

When discussing cloud serve providers and cloud capabilities, the public cloud tends to be the solution to which is being referred most often. All cloud resources are owned by the provider and offered to the general public through lease or contract agreements. The decision to utilize public cloud services will change from entity to entity based on existing infrastructure and organizational needs. Listed below are six examples of public cloud providers a BCP manager will mostly likely encounter when researching cloud-based solutions.

1. Microsoft Azure
2. Amazon Web Services (AWS)
3. Rackspace Managed Cloud
4. Google Cloud Platform (G-Suite)

5. IBM Cloud
6. Oracle Cloud
7. Alibaba Cloud

Private Cloud

Private clouds are owned and operated by individual organizations for the specific use of their staff, customers, and vendors. They are based on standard IT legacy environments of datacenters and all supporting infrastructure. Staff, customers, and vendors can connect to an organizations' private cloud through the Internet with a web browser using a remote access capability.

The configuration of the private cloud will change from entity to entity based on existing infrastructure and services needed. Formerly referred to as "intranets," private clouds are typically used for shared storage and internal resources such as a hosted SharePoint solution. Listed below are five use cases for private cloud a BCP manager should be aware of when considering this option.

1. Potential Cost Savings
2. Agile Development Environment
3. Deployment of Production Workloads
4. Enhanced Flexibility and Transparency
5. Control over Security and Compliance

Community Cloud

Community clouds provide infrastructure and functionality that is owned and operated by affinity groups and similar organizations. Segments are owned and maintained by individual organizations, while the responsibility of joint tasks and functions are assumed by the group as a whole. Examples of community cloud solutions can be found in online gaming communities. Listed below are examples of how constituent members of a community cloud such as PlayStation would interface and interact at various levels.

1. *PlayStation*: The Network Umbrella Unit
2. *Sony*: Hosts the Network IAM Functionality

3. *Game Vendors*: Host DRM Servers
4. *End Users*: Conduct Testing and Processing

Hybrid Cloud

Hybrid clouds contain elements of public, private, and community cloud models to varying degrees based on customer needs. In this model, private cloud resources are retained—such as the organizations' legacy infrastructure—as well as legacy production environments for operations. Applications and software are retained for specific use by staff, customers, and vendors and accessed remotely.

The organization leases space on the public cloud (typically a PaaS model) for software development. This hybrid model protects the legacy production environment and exposes associated systems to less risk of harm.

The Role of Cloud Computing in Disaster Planning

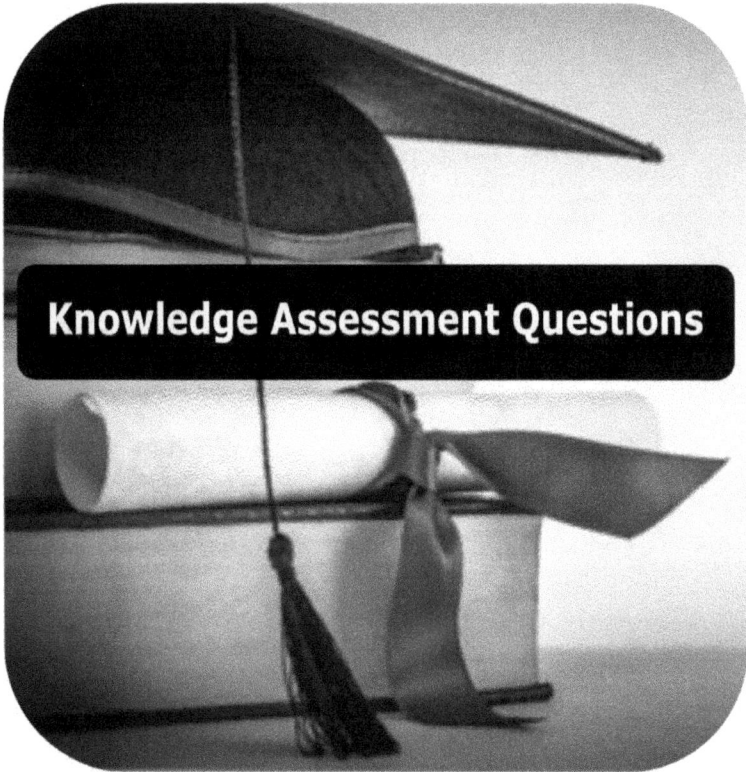

Knowledge Assessment Questions

The following knowledge assessment questions are presented as true / false, multiple choice, and fill-in-the-blank. The correct answers are provided in an Answer Key at the end of the text. These questions may or may not be presented on the actual certification exam.

Domain 09: Knowledge Assessment Questions

1. Which choice below does **not** qualify as one of the five established characteristics of cloud computing?

A. On-Demand Self-Service

B. Resource Pooling

C. Incremental Rigidity

D. Measured Service (Metering)

E. None of the Above

2. Hybrid clouds contain elements of public, private, and community cloud models to varying degrees based on _____.

A. Customer Needs

B. Provider Capability

C. Geographic Location

D. Staffing Capacity

E. None of the Above

3. Which choice below describes the services offered to customers using Hybrid Cloud solutions?

A. Private Cloud Resources Retained

B. Legacy Production Environment Retained

C. Public Cloud Space is Leased

D. Accessed Remotely by End Users

E. All of the Above

4. Community clouds provide infrastructure and _____ that is owned and operated by affinity groups and similar organizations.

A. Benefits

B. Functionality

C. Savings

D. Efficiency

E. None of the Above

5. Which choice below is **not** one of the actions taken when determining an organizations' existing operational state?

A. Interview Internal End Users

B. Interview External Customers

C. Interview Unit Managers

D. Interview Cloud Providers

E. None of the Above

6. In the PaaS model, the cloud service provider offers not only the IaaS capability but provides the customer with _____ as well.

A. Software Licenses

B. Cloud Contracts

C. Operating Systems

D. Volume Data Plans

E. None of the Above

7. Which choice below is not a service offered to customers by Private Cloud Providers?

A. Cloud Resources Owned by Provider

B. Rented or Leased to Customers

C. Segments Owned by Organizations

D. No Remote Access Capabilities

E. All of the Above

8. Managing data and its required infrastructure is neither a core function of most organizations nor is it a _____ to the business process.

A. Profit Center

B. Requirement

C. Critical Task

D. Priority

E. None of the Above

9. Which choice below is **not** a valid reason for an organization to consider migrating from a legacy system to a cloud solution?

A. Service Costs Not Included in Cloud Contract

B. IT Staff are Typically Expensive

C. Recruiting and Retention are Difficult

D. Cloud Reduces the Need for IT Personnel

E. None of the Above

10. Cloud services are typically offered in _____ models based on provider capability and customer needs.

A. Five

B. Four

C. Two

D. Three

E. None of the Above

11. Which choice below is **not** a characteristic that cloud customers will experience using the Software as a Service (SaaS) model?

A. Provider Maintains All Software

B. Customer Uploads and Processes Data

C. Customer Provides Operating System

D. A Hosted Full Production Environment

E. None of the Above

12. Despite many functions and configurations, _____ is one of the five characteristics officially accepted as part of the cloud computing definition.

A. User Friendly

B. Measured Service

C. Financially Stable

D. Data Driven

E. None of the Above

13. Despite many functions and configurations, NIST lists ten characteristics that are accepted as part of the cloud computing definition.

1. True

2. False

14. Hybrid clouds contain elements of public, private, and community cloud models to varying degrees based on customer needs.

1. True

2. False

15. Organizations tend to underutilize a technical resource (potential failure) or overutilize a technical resource (wasted money).

1. True

2. False

16. Private clouds are owned and operated by individual organizations for the specific use of their staff, customers, and vendors.

1. True

2. False

17. Unless organizations use a cloud environment, they cannot transfer the risk or liability associated with disclosure of Personally Identifiable Information (PII).

1. True

2. False

18. In the Software as a Service (SaaS) model, the customer receives all the underlying IaaS and PaaS capabilities, as well as end user applications.

1. True

2. False

DOMAIN 10

Cloud Data
Storage and Security

Domain 10: *Cloud Data Storage and Security*

Cloud Data Life Cycle (CDLC)

Data stored in the cloud tends to have the same needs as data stored in legacy systems and should be treated in the same manner. Listed below are the six stages of the *Cloud Data Life Cycle* that demonstrate its similarity to the data life cycle in legacy systems.

1. *Create* Data
2. *Store* Data
3. *Use* Data
4. *Share* Data
5. *Archive* Data
6. *Delete* Data

CDLC: Create Data

Users can create data by accessing the cloud remotely or from within the cloud datacenter where the data resides. The means by which users create data will change from entity to entity based on organizational structure and policy. Whether data is created remotely or from within the cloud environment, the practices of information security will apply. Listed below are four principles typically implemented by users creating data in the cloud.

1. Encrypt the Data Prior to Uploading
2. Use a Cryptosystem with a High Work Factor
3. Use a Cryptosystem Listed on FIPS 140-2
4. Secure the Upload Connection (VPN, IPSec)

CDLC: Use Data

Operations within a cloud environment will require remote access with secured connections (typically an encrypted tunnel) utilized in such a way that the cloud provider cannot access raw client data. Users relying on remote access must be aware of potential risks and trained in the use of the technology needed to mitigate those risks. Users must also be informed of any and all VPN, DRM, and/or DLP requirements when interfacing with data. Leadership must be made aware that logging and audit trails are crucial in this environment, and strong protections using virtualization are strongly encouraged.

CDLC: Share Data

Global collaboration is a powerful capability of the cloud, but the risks associated with that power are global as well. The fact that cloud users can be anywhere means threats can be anywhere as well. The means by which users share data will change from entity to entity based on organizational policy and location. The ability to share data in the cloud may be restricted by jurisdictional law, or by regulatory mandates. Listed below are three practices typically implemented when sharing data in cloud environments.

1. Encrypt all Files and Communications
2. Utilize Digital Rights Management Solutions
3. Utilize Export and Import Controls for Technology

CDLC: Archive Data

Archived data is stored for long periods of time, and these longer timeframes will tend to require special security considerations. When data is archived for BCP/DRP purposes cryptography is an essential component, key management is crucial, and the physical security of the data is equally as important. The means by which archived data is stored will change from entity to entity based on organizational policy and location. Listed below are four questions a BCP manager should ask when archiving data in the cloud.

1. Where is the Data Stored?
2. What Format is Used for Data Storage?
3. Who is Staffing the Storage Location?
4. What Data Transfer Procedures Exist?

Cloud Architecture: Volume Storage

There are two primary data storage methods associated with cloud architecture: *volume storage* and *object-based storage*. With the volume storage option, cloud customers are assigned storage space that is typically attached to a virtual machine. It uses allocated blocks for file-based storage that share the same hierarchy and structure as that found in legacy systems. Listed below are characteristics typically associated with volume storage which should be known before considering this storage method.

1. The Allocated Volume can Contain Anything
2. It has Higher Flexibility and Performance
3. It has More Administrative Overhead
4. This Method is Typically Used with IaaS Solutions

Cloud Architecture: Object-Based Storage

With an *object-based storage* solution, data is stored individually as objects as opposed to files or blocks. The data stored as objects includes not only production content, but extensive metadata for the content as well. The stored objects share a similarity with database objects as they are each assigned a unique address identifier. Listed below are four characteristics typically associated with object-based storage which should be known before considering this storage method.

1. Allows for Marking, Labels and Classification
2. Enhances Data Indexing Capabilities
3. Enhances Data Policy Enforcement
4. Allows for Centralized Data Management

Content Delivery Network (CDN)

A *content delivery network* (CDN) is a form of data caching typically located near geophysical locations of predicted high demand and use. Using this method data is not drawn from a datacenter; the CDN stores copies of media based on likelihood of user requests.

This accommodates users at varying distances by allowing for increased bandwidth and delivery quality. The implementation the CDN will change from entity to entity based on organizational policy and location, but it will typically be used for online multimedia streaming services.

Cloud Data Security: Encryption

Like its legacy environment counterpart, cloud computing solutions have a significant dependency on encryption to operate. In fact, no encryption would mean no cloud service. The client enterprise uses encryption to protect its data, and the cloud service provider uses encryption to isolate client data from other clients in a shared resource environment. Listed below are the four primary functions of encryption typically encountered in cloud environments.

1. Create Secure Remote Connections
2. Protect Data at Rest
3. Protect Data in Use
4. Protect Data in Transit

Cloud Data Security: Key Management

The methods and locations chosen to manage encrypted keys impacts the risk to data in several ways. The implementation of a key management will change from entity to entity based on organizational policy and need. In some instances, an organization may decide to outsource its key management program to a third party such as a *Cloud Access Security Broker* (CASB). In other cases, the key management may remain an internal responsibility. Regardless of the method chosen to manage encrypted keys there are five common areas of concern that must be considered and addressed.

1. Level of Protection Implemented
2. Creation of a Key Recovery Policy
3. Creation of a Key Distribution Policy
4. Creation of a Key Revocation Policy
5. Creation of a Key Escrow Policy

Obfuscation, Masking, and Anonymization

In certain instances, customers using cloud provider solutions may find it necessary to obscure data and use a representation of data instead. This is not considered to be a "best practice" within the information security field but there times when these measures become necessary. The choice of using obfuscation, masking, and anonymization as a method for information security will change from entity to entity based on organizational policy and need. This can be a viable option if supporting security controls are put in place such as "sandboxing" for test environments, least privilege enforcement within the network, and the establishment of a secure remote access policy for all users with access to the data. Listed below are four examples of obfuscation, masking, and anonymization typically implemented by organizations within their information security program.

1. Hashing (One-Way Function)
2. Randomization (Replacement of Data)
3. Masking (Hiding Data with Data)
4. Shuffling (Randomization Using Production Data)

Security Information and Event Management

To better collect, manage, analyze, and display log data, a set of SIEM tools have been developed specifically for that purpose. SIEM is an approach to security management that combines SIM (security information management) and SEM (security event management) functions into one security management system. The underlying principles of every SIEM system is to aggregate relevant data from multiple sources, identify deviations from the norm and take appropriate action.

One of the primary drivers for SIEM solutions is that humans are not very efficient at long-term analysis of logs. When an individual spends too much time analyzing logs the information tends to blend together and events may be overlooked. When someone spends too little time analyzing logs a knowledge and experience gap is created that leads to the same result of missed events. The choice of using a SIEM solution as a method for information security will change from entity to entity based on organizational policy and need.

The choice to implement a SIEM solution is not entirely without risk: aggregated data is stored in one location making it vulnerable to compromise. In spite of this risk there are many benefits to the implementation of a SEIM solution, six of which are listed below.

Domain 10: *Cloud Data Storage and Security*

1. Centralized Collection of Log Data
2. Enhanced Log Analysis Capabilities
3. Trend Detection in Large Datasets
4. Dashboarding (Management Display)
5. Automated Response Capabilities
6. Data Storage and Normalization

Data Loss Prevention: Egress Monitoring

An egress monitoring solution will examine data leaving the production environment and react based on preestablished rules and parameters. It is usually implemented as an additional layer of security for the purpose of *Data Loss Prevention* (DLP). The choice of using a DLP solution and the data to be monitored will change from entity to entity based on organizational policy and need. Listed below are five functions of egress monitoring that may offer an organization the benefit of an additional security control.

1. Prevents the Inadvertent or Malicious Disclosure of Data
2. Serves as a Policy Enforcement Mechanism
3. Provides Enhanced Monitoring Capabilities
4. Creates an Enhanced Capability for Regulatory Compliance
5. Establishes a Higher Level of Data Dissemination Control

DOMAIN 10

Cloud Data
Storage and Security

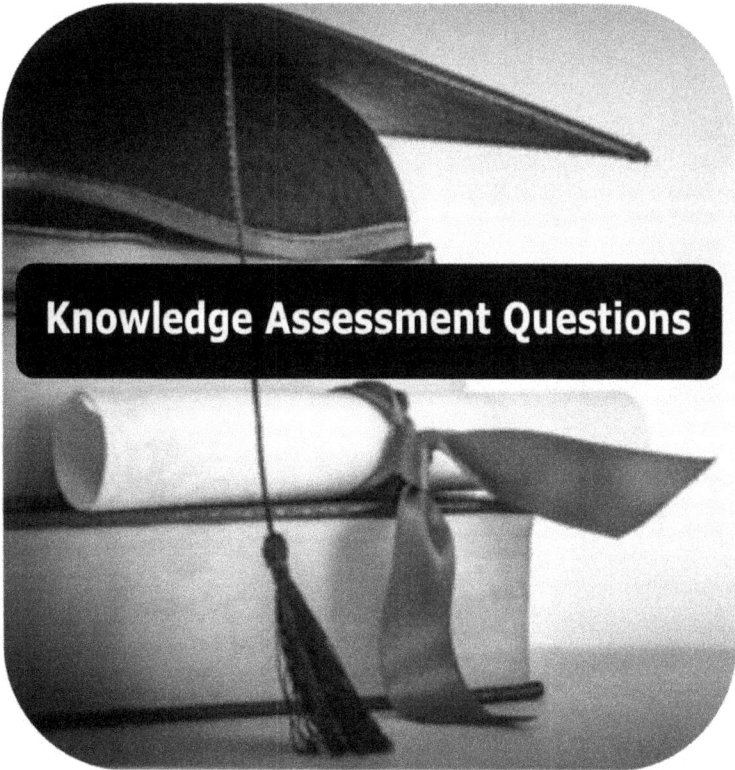

Knowledge Assessment Questions

The following knowledge assessment questions are presented as true / false, multiple choice, and fill-in-the-blank. The correct answers are provided in an Answer Key at the end of the text. These questions may or may not be presented on the actual certification exam.

Domain 10: Knowledge Assessment Questions

1. There are six defined phases in the Cloud Data Life Cycle. What phase immediately follows the "store" phase?

A. Create

B. Use

C. Share

D. Archive

E. None of the Above

2. Despite many functions and configurations, _____ is one of the five characteristics officially accepted as part of the cloud computing definition.

A. User Friendly

B. Measured Service

C. Financially Stable

D. Data Driven

E. None of the Above

3. Which option below is **not** a characteristic or action associated with the "Create Data" phase in the Cloud Development Life Cycle?

A. Data Created in Cloud by User

B. Use a Cryptosystem Listed on FIPS 140-2

C. Use a Cryptosystem with a Low Work Factor

D. Data is Encrypted Before Uploading

E. None of the Above

4. When considering cloud architecture, _____ is one of the key characteristics of the volume storage model.

A. Higher Flexibility and Performance

B. Unique Address Identifier Assigned

C. Marking, Labels and Classification

D. Enhances Data Policy Enforcement

E. None of the Above

5. Which option below is **not** a benefit or characteristic of "Egress Monitoring" when considering the implementation of a Data Loss Prevention solution?

A. Data Assimilation Control Mechanism

B. Enhanced Layer of Security

C. Enhanced Regulatory Compliance

D. Policy Enforcement Mechanism

E. None of the Above

6. When considering cloud architecture, _____ is one of the key characteristics of the object-based storage model.

A. Allocated Volume Contains Anything

B. More Administrative Overhead

C. Centralized Data Management

D. Typically Used with IaaS Solutions

E. None of the Above

7. Which option below presents the **least** attractive Cloud Data Security option when considering the topic of Obfuscation, Masking and Anonymization?

A. Masking

B. Shuffling

C. Least Privilege Enforcement

D. Randomization

E. None of the Above

8. A(n) _____ is a form of data caching typically located near geophysical locations of high demand and use.

A. Personal Area Network

B. Virtual Private Network

C. Storage Area Network

D. Content Delivery Network

E. None of the Above

9. Which option below is **not** a characteristic or action associated with the "Share Data" phase in the Cloud Development Life Cycle?

A. Critical Files and Communications are Encrypted

B. May be Sharing Restrictions by Jurisdiction

C. May be Restrictions from Regulatory Mandates

D. User Anywhere = Threats Everywhere

E. None of the Above

10. In certain instances, customers using cloud provider solutions may find it necessary to _____ data and use a representation of data instead.

A. Delete

B. Obscure

C. Backup

D. Archive

E. None of the Above

11. Which option below is **not** a characteristic or action associated with "Volume Storage" when considering the structure of Cloud architecture?

A. File-Based Storage

B. Same Hierarchy / Structure as Legacy System

C. Lower Administrative Overhead

D. Typically Used with IaaS Solutions

E. None of the Above

12. A(n) _____ monitoring solution will examine data leaving the production environment and react based on preestablished rules and parameters.

A. Egress

B. Firewall

C. IDS

D. IPS

E. None of the Above

13. Data stored in the cloud tends to have different needs as data stored in legacy systems and should be treated in a unique and proper manner.

1. True

2. False

14. An egress monitoring solution will examine data leaving the production environment and react based on preestablished rules and parameters.

1. True

2. False

15. Operations within a legacy environment will require remote access with secured connections (typically a username and password).

1. True

2. False

16. In certain instances, customers using cloud provider solutions may find it necessary to obscure data and use a representation of data instead.

1. True

2. False

17. Archived data is stored for long periods of time; longer timeframes will tend to reduce the requirement for special security considerations.

1. True

2. False

18. Like its legacy environment counterpart, cloud computing solutions have a significant dependency on encryption to operate.

1. True

2. False

DOMAIN 11

Cloud Security
Risks and Threat Vectors

Cloud Platform Risks

Because the cloud customer and provider will each process data, they will share responsibilities and risks associated with the data. In the event of unauthorized use or disclosure of PII, the provider may be financial liable for damages if that responsibility is codified in the service contract. Although the customer may recover the financial losses stipulated in the contract, the customer assumes all responsibility and ownership of criminal and civil liabilities.

In addition, if the customer is protected by the providers' acceptance of financial responsibility, legal repercussions are not the only negative impact on the organization. Listed below are five impacts likely to be experienced by the customer while the litigation process works its way through the legal system.

1. Negative Publicity
2. Loss of Clientele Faith
3. Decrease in Market Share
4. Decrease in Share Value (Publicly Held Organizations)
5. Increase in Insurance Costs

Private Cloud Risks

A private cloud configuration is a legacy configuration of a datacenter with distributed computing capabilities. There are no risks unique to private clouds that do not impact other platforms. The benefit of a private cloud as relating to risk is the organization retains complete control over the cloud environment, making any response much timelier and more efficient.

Listed below are five categories of risk typically considered by organizations utilizing a private cloud solution.

1. Personnel Threats
2. Natural Disasters
3. External Threats
4. Regulatory and Compliance Risks
5. Malware Risks (Internal and External)

Community Cloud Risks

In a community cloud configuration, resources are allocated, shared, and dispersed among affinity groups. This provides the members of the platform several benefits, but each of those benefits presents a risk to the cloud customer. The community cloud has shared ownership; if one node becomes unavailable the others will continue to operate. However, each node in a shared environment also presents itself as a unique point of entry. Costs are shared and distributed, but the responsibility for access and overall control of the environment is shared as well. This also removes the need for centralized administration but at the same time denies members the reliability of centralized standards.

Public Cloud Risks

In a public cloud configuration, a company offers cloud services to any entity wanting to become a cloud customer. While this option poses the same risks as those impacting private and community clouds, it also exposes the customer to risks unique to this specific environment. Listed below are six risks typically experienced by customers that are unique to public cloud platforms.

1. The Customer Loses Control of Data
2. The Customer Loses Oversight of Operations
3. The Customer Loses all Audit Ability of Data and Systems
4. The Customer Loses the Ability to Enforce Policy
5. The Customer Risks the Potential of Vendor Lock-In
6. The Customer Risks the Potential of Vendor Lock-Out

Vendor Lock-Out

Vendor lock-out can be caused when the provider goes out of business, is acquired by another interest, or ceases operation for any reason. This risk is rare but still must be considered. Listed below are five public cloud provider characteristics the BCP manager should consider when assessing potential risk.

1. The Providers' Longevity

2. The Providers' Core Competency
3. The Providers' Jurisdictional Suitability
4. The Providers' Supply Chain Dependencies
5. The Legislative Environment for the Provider and Client

Risks: IaaS (Infrastructure as a Service)

In the IaaS (Infrastructure as a Service) model, the customer will have the most control over its resources. Only the infrastructure (hardware) is maintained and administered by the provider; the customer manages all other aspects of the cloud operation. This level of control presents the organization with potential risks. The risks associated with the IaaS model will change from entity to entity based on organizational structure and staffing. Listed below are six potential areas of risk that should be considered by the BCP manager conducting a risk assessment or analysis of this model.

1. Personnel Threats
2. External Threats
3. Lack of Required Skillsets (Organizational Staff)
4. All Access will be by Remote Connection
5. Responsibility for all Operational and Security Functions
6. Lack of Sufficient Personnel to Manage Solution

Risks: PaaS (Platform as a Service)

In the PaaS (Platform as a Service) model, the customer will have all the risks associated with the IaaS model as well as additional risks specific to the PaaS model. The risks associated with the PaaS model will change from entity to entity based on organizational structure and staffing. Listed below are three potential areas of risk that should be considered by the BCP manager conducting a risk assessment or analysis of this model.

1. **Interoperability Issues**: The PaaS model requires the provider to provide, administer and update the operating systems required by the customer. Issues may arise when unannounced version and/or patch management actions are initiated by the provider but unknown to the customer. This may impact critical software functionality and APS's.

2. **Persistent Backdoors**: A benefit of the PaaS model is that it allows software developers (DevOps) to create and test software in non-production environment. In many cases developers install persistent backdoors in the software to ease the burden of making iterative changes anywhere in the process. If this software is transferred to a production environment without removing these backdoors, today's DevOps project may become tomorrow's zero-day exploit.

3. **Virtualization Risks**: Most virtualization solutions utilized by cloud customers reside on resources shared by other cloud customers. Potential risks such as information bleed and side-channel attacks can occur if virtualization security controls are not effective. Unfortunately for the cloud customer, they have no ability to attenuate these potential risks, and must rely entirely on the provider to ensure these risks are recognized and mitigated.

Risks: SaaS (Software as a Service)

In the SaaS (Software as a Service) model, the customer will have all the IaaS and PaaS risks listed above as well as risks specific to the SaaS model. In this model the customer has almost no control the cloud environment and must be especially vigilant when conducting operations. The risks associated with the SaaS model will change from entity to entity based on organizational structure and software utilization. Listed below are five potential areas of risk that should be considered by the BCP manager conducting a risk assessment or analysis of the SaaS model.

1. Customer Data Stored in Proprietary Formats
2. Virtualization Risks Cannot be Attenuated by the Customer
3. Web Application Security Issues
4. Customer Access is Required Solely via Web Browser
5. Potential Weaknesses in API's Disrupting Applications

Virtualization Risks

As stated in the previous sections, many potential threats are posed by virtualization in public cloud environments that can only be attenuated via the use of controls that can only be implemented by the cloud service provider. An attack on the hypervisor is the most serious of those concerns. The risks associated with the virtualization will change from entity to entity based on organizational structure and virtualization architecture.

Malicious actors tend to prefer Type II hypervisors—those that reside on top of an operating system as opposed to residing on bare metal (a Type I hypervisor)—because the associated operating system provides a much greater attack surface. The Type II configuration is typically used by cloud providers for their customers. Listed below are five potential areas of risk that should be considered by the BCP manager conducting a risk assessment or analysis of a virtualization implementation.

1. Guest Escape
2. Host Escape (Rare, but Possible)
3. Information Bleed (Shared Resources)
4. Identification of Process-Specific Information
5. Data Seizure by Law Enforcement (Collateral Damage)

Private Cloud Threats

Although many threats to cloud computing are the same as those faced in legacy operations, they may manifest in novel ways and present new risks. The threats associated with private cloud solutions will change from entity to entity based on organizational policies and system architecture.

Listed below are seven potential threats that should be considered by the BCP manager conducting a risk assessment or analysis of a private cloud platform.

1. Internal Threats (and External Contractors)
2. External Attackers
3. Man-in-the-Middle Attacks
4. Increased Exposure via Remote Access Capability
5. Social Engineering
6. Theft and/or Loss of Devices (BYOD Environments)
7. Regulatory and Compliance Violations

Domain 11: *Cloud Security Risks and Threat Vectors*

Public Cloud Threats

The public cloud not only includes all threats associated with private clouds but includes threats totally outside the customers' ability to defend against and control. These threats can cause more damage in cloud environments than they would in legacy systems. Additionally, two sets of governance and guidelines—the providers' and the customers'—hinder the process of securing permission to resolve certain issues.

To perform their work effectively, technicians may be inclined to conduct unapproved operations at a higher rate under these restrictions. Listed below are three potential threats that should be considered by the BCP manager conducting a risk assessment or analysis of a public cloud platform even if they cannot be controlled.

1. Rogue Administrators
2. Escalation of Privileges
3. Contractual Failure (Unlikely, but Possible)

Cloud-Specific BIA Risks

Unlike a legacy environment, a customer conducting operations in the cloud will not be able to conduct local computing without the provider (unless the cloud platform is a hybrid). The BIA must also consider a new set of upstream and downstream for the cloud service as well. The ease of data distribution and storage across diverse geographical locations presents an additional set of regulatory and compliance risks.

Additionally, the inclusion of internal personnel and increased remote access elevate the threat of data breaches and unauthorized disclosures of PII. Finally, the risks of both vendor lock-in and vendor lock-out must also be considered when assessing cloud computing for BCP needs.

DOMAIN 11

Cloud Security
Risks and Threat Vectors

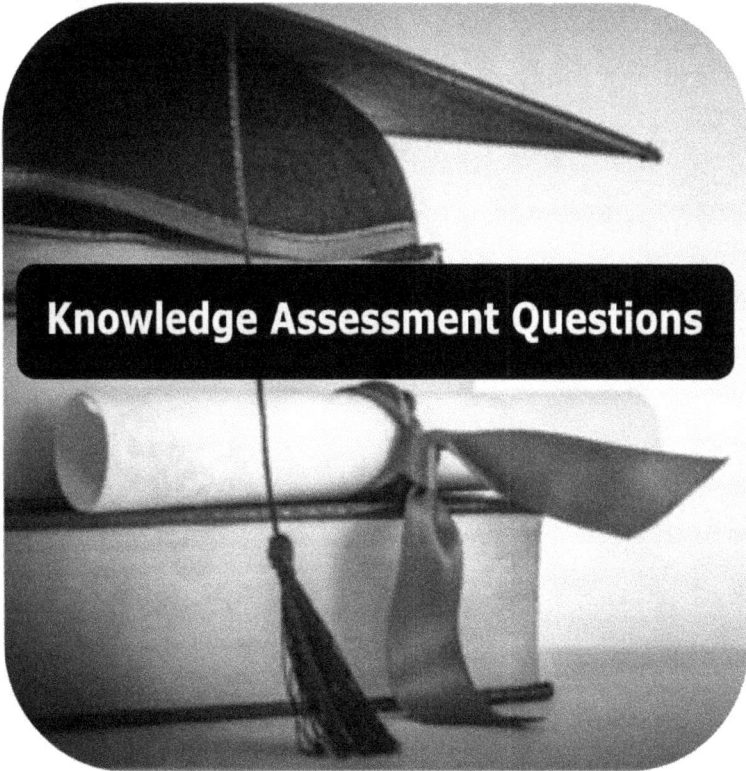

Knowledge Assessment Questions

The following knowledge assessment questions are presented as true / false, multiple choice, and fill-in-the-blank. The correct answers are provided in an Answer Key at the end of the text. These questions may or may not be presented on the actual certification exam.

Domain 11: Knowledge Assessment Questions

1. Which option below is **not** a characteristic or action associated with Cloud Platform Risks?

A. Provider is Financially Liable

B. Provider Owns Civil Liability

C. Customer Owns Criminal Liability

D. Codified in Service Agreement

E. None of the Above

2. A _____ configuration is a legacy configuration of a datacenter with distributed computing capabilities.

A. Hybrid Cloud

B. Community Cloud

C. Public Cloud

D. Private Cloud

E. None of the Above

3. Which option below is **not** a characteristic or actions associated with a Private Cloud when considering data security risks?

A. Regulatory and Compliance Risks

B. Internal / External Threats

C. Natural / Manmade Disasters

D. Reduced Organizational Control

E. None of the Above

4. A _____ configuration is one in which resources are allocated, shared, and dispersed among affinity groups.

A. Hybrid Cloud

B. Community Cloud

C. Public Cloud

D. Private Cloud

E. None of the Above

5. Which option below is **not** a characteristic or action associated with the Public Cloud when considering data security risks?

A. Customer Loses Audit Ability

B. Same Risks as Private Cloud

C. Customer Loses Enforcement Ability

D. Customer Loses Control

E. None of the Above

6. A _____ configuration is one in which a company offers cloud services to any entity wanting to become a cloud customer.

A. Hybrid Cloud

B. Community Cloud

C. Public Cloud

D. Private Cloud

E. None of the Above

7. Which option below is **not** a characteristic or action associated with data security risks when considering utilizing the Platform as a Service (PaaS) model in a Public Cloud?

A. Interoperability Issues

B. Resources Shared by Customers

C. O/S Administered by Customer

D. Virtualization Risks

E. None of the Above

8. Many potential threats posed by _____ require attenuation via the use of controls that can only be implemented by the provider.

A. Virtualization

B. Malware

C. Malicious Actors

D. Web Browsers

E. None of the Above

9. Which option below is **not** a characteristic or action associated with data security risks when considering utilizing virtualization capabilities in a Public Cloud?

A. Attackers Execute a Guest Escape

B. Data Seizure by Law Enforcement

C. Attackers Execute a Host Escape

D. Attackers Prefer Type 1 Hypervisors

E. None of the Above

10. Unlike a legacy environment, a customer conducting operations in the cloud will not be able to conduct _____ without the provider.

A. Business Operations

B. Vulnerability Assessments

C. Risk Assessments

D. Local Computing

E. None of the Above

11. Which option below is **not** a characteristic or action associated with data security risks when considering utilizing a Private Cloud environment?

A. Theft or Loss of Devices (BYOD)

B. Man-in-the-Middle Attacks

C. Regulatory Violations

D. Social Engineering

E. None of the Above

12. _____ can be caused when the provider goes out of business, is acquired by another interest, or ceases operation for any reason.

A. Vendor Lock-In

B. Jurisdictional Issues

C. Vendor Lock-Out

D. Regulatory Failure

E. None of the Above

13. Because the cloud customer and provider will each process data, they will share responsibilities and risks associated with the data.

1. True
2. False

14. Unlike a legacy environment, a customer conducting operations in the cloud will be able to conduct limited local computing without the provider.

1. True
2. False

15. A private cloud configuration is a legacy configuration of a datacenter with associated distributed computing capabilities.

1. True
2. False

16. Although many threats to cloud computing are the same faced in legacy operations, they manifest in the same way and present the same types of risk.

1. True
2. False

17. In a public cloud configuration, a company offers cloud services to any entity wanting to become a cloud customer.

1. True
2. False

18. In the Software as a Service (SaaS) model, the customer will only have the Platform as a Service (PaaS) model risks and responsibilities.

1. True
2. False

DOMAIN 12

Cloud Security
Responsibility and Administration

Foundations of Managed Cloud Services

Some element of adversarial relationship exists between the cloud customer and the provider because they have somewhat different goals. For these reason, contracts and Service Level Agreements are crucial components of a stable relationship. The "gray areas" not formally defined by a contract are where this risk for both parties exists. Listed below are five examples of differences between customers and providers in the goals of their relationship.

1. Customer: Seeks to Maximize Operational Capabilities
2. Customer: Seeks to Maximize Data Security
3. Customer: Seeks to Minimize Operational Expenses
4. Provider: Seeks to Maximize Profits
5. Provider: Seeks to Minimize Service Labor for Customer

Provider: Physical Plant

The provider is responsible for the administration of the physical plant. The physical plant of the datacenter will include the facility campus, all physical components, and the services that support them. Responsibilities for administration of the physical plant will change from provider to provider based on organizational structure and needs. Listed below are seven areas of provider responsibility typically associated with administration of the physical plant for the cloud customer.

1. Ensure the Use of Secure Hardware Components
2. Ensure the Use of TPM Standards for BIOS Firmware
3. Ensure the Use of a Managed Hardware Configuration
4. Establish Controls for Logging Events and Incidents
5. Establish Policies for Incidents, Forensics, and Attribution
6. Maintain all Components for Customer Needs
7. Ensure Configuration for Secure Remote Access

Provider: Secure Logical Framework

In addition to securing the hardware components, the cloud provider must ensure that the logical elements are equally protected. The provider must take all reasonable steps to prevent data leakage and malicious aggregation of the customer data. The steps taken to secure the providers' logical framework will change from provider to provider based on organizational structure and capability. Listed below are five areas of provider responsibility typically associated with securing logical elements for the cloud customer.

1. Ensure the Use of Virtual Operating Systems
2. Ensure the Use of Virtualization Management Tools
3. Ensure Configuration Policy Enforcement
4. Ensure the Configuration of VM Elements is Secure
5. Ensure the Attenuation of Potential Risks

Provider: Secure Networking

Secure networking often involves the same tactics and methods used in legacy environments, but with cloud-specific permutations. The steps taken to secure the customers' network will change from provider to provider based on organizational structure and needs. Listed below are seven categories of security controls typically implemented when securing networks for the cloud customer.

1. Firewalls
2. IDS / IPS
3. Honeypots
4. Use of Vulnerability Assessments
5. Systems to Protect Secure Communication
6. Use of Encryption and Strong Authentication
7. Use of *Virtual Private Networks* (VPN's)

Provider: Mapping and Selection of Controls

The cloud provider must apply the proper security controls according to a customers' relevant regulatory frameworks and planned usage. A "one size fits all" mentality will never be an effective approach. The provider must create and make available published governance guides, and its subsequent security policies must be based on the published governance guides. All security controls selected and implemented by the provider must be justified by recognized industry standards, such as those found in the CSA's *Cloud Controls Matrix* (cloudsecurityalliance.org). Additionally, the controls selected and implemented must be equally applicable to both the customers' needs and the providers' datacenter.

Shared Responsibilities by Service Type

By reviewing the type of service model utilized by the customer, the responsibilities can be shared and assigned to the appropriate party. Listed below are the three primary cloud service models and the level of shared responsibility typically associated with each.

1. **IaaS** (Infrastructure as a Service): The provider is responsible for the physical security of the plant and infrastructure, and the customer is responsible for all other functionality and services that follow.

2. **PaaS** (Platform as a Service): The provider is responsible for the physical security of the plant, the infrastructure, and the administration and security of all operating systems. The customer is responsible for all other functionality and services that follow.

3. **SaaS** (Software as a Service): The provider is responsible for the physical security of the plant, the infrastructure, the administration and security of all operating systems, and the administration and security of all software and applications utilized by the customer. The customer is responsible for assigning access and permissions to those services for vendors, staff, and customers.

Shared Responsibility: O/S Management

The operating system is a large attack surface and offers many potential vectors to malicious actors if not secured correctly. Even with a PaaS model in which the provider assumes responsibility for administration of the operating systems, there are several ways in which the provider and customer may collaborate to manage their security. Listed below are seven areas in which the provider and customer can work together and manage the security of the O/S.

1. Removing Unnecessary Services
2. Closing Unused Ports
3. Installing Antimalware Agents
4. Limiting Administrator Access
5. Removing Default Accounts and Passwords
6. Enabling System Event and Incident Logging
7. Creating a Formal Approval Process for Deviations

Shared Responsibility: Data Access

In all cloud service models, the customer and their users will need to access and modify the data at various levels. This another area in which cloud customers and providers can share responsibility and support each other. Listed below are methods by which the cloud customers and providers secure access to customer data.

1. **Customer Administration**: In this model, the customer has complete control and responsibility for data access in the cloud. This is always the case in IaaS (Infrastructure as a Service) models, as the customer assumes responsibility for the operating system and all associated security controls.

2. **Provider Administration**: In this model, the customer and the provider share the responsibility for data access. This requires good communication between both parties. The requests for access will be made through the provider, who then confirms with the customer (via automation) that the requests are legitimate.

3. **Third-Party Administration**: In this model, the customer and provider both work with a *cloud access security broker* (CASB) to manage data access. The CASB works with the customer and provider to verify user accounts and ensure the access requests are legitimate.

Lack of Physical Access

The cloud provider will not have any reason to allow the customer any physical access to the facility containing customer data. This is both a challenging and beneficial situation for both parties. The cloud providers have every reason not to grant access to customers. The provider may work with thousands of customers, each of them having various levels of trust. Additionally, the more a customer knows about the internal operations of the provider, the higher degree of risk exists of that knowledge being exploited.

This lack of access can be beneficial insofar that it builds customer trust in the cloud providers' security. After all, every customer is denied access equally for security purposes. The challenge of this lack of access is that the customer must rely on the providers' assertions of security controls without the ability to validate or verify those assertions firsthand.

Lack of Auditing Ability

The cloud providers' unwillingness to allow customer access to the facility applies to the customers' auditors as well. The challenge exists with situations in which the cloud customer must demonstrate they are meeting regulatory and compliance requirements for data storage. This can also be frustrating for key stakeholders requiring audit results from the company.

In response to this challenge, cloud customers and providers agree through use of service contracts to rely on licensed and chartered auditors to conduct required audits that satisfy both parties. These third parties publish "audit assurance statements" that are then made available to the customer and the provider. Different levels of audit assurance statements are made available for audiences with different needs. Listed below are the three types of *SOC* (System and Organization Controls) reports typically encountered by individuals concerned with audit assurance.

1. **SOC 01**: This report falls completely within the domain of financial reporting and has no applicability to security in the cloud.

2. **SOC 02**: This report contains comprehensive details of the cloud provider audit and is never released to the public for security reasons.

3. **SOC 03**: This report is a brief audit assertion, based on the comprehensive audit, that is released to customers and the public. This is based on the *transitive model of trust*. If A (provider) trusts B (auditor), and if C (customer) trusts B (auditor), then by extension C (customer) will trust A (provider). That is the general theory as to why SOC 03 reports satisfy regulatory and compliance requirements.

Shared Responsibility: Monitoring and Testing

An area where cloud providers and customers may find common ground in sharing responsibilities is in security monitoring and testing. The provider may allow the customer remote access to conduct testing in support of its own testing initiatives, but the access will be very restricted.

The granting of limited access to a customer by a provider must be stipulated in a service contract. Limiting the customer to specific aspects of the providers' system reduces the risk of significant harm to the infrastructure, and this of data disclosure within shared resources.

Cloud Security Responsibility and Administration

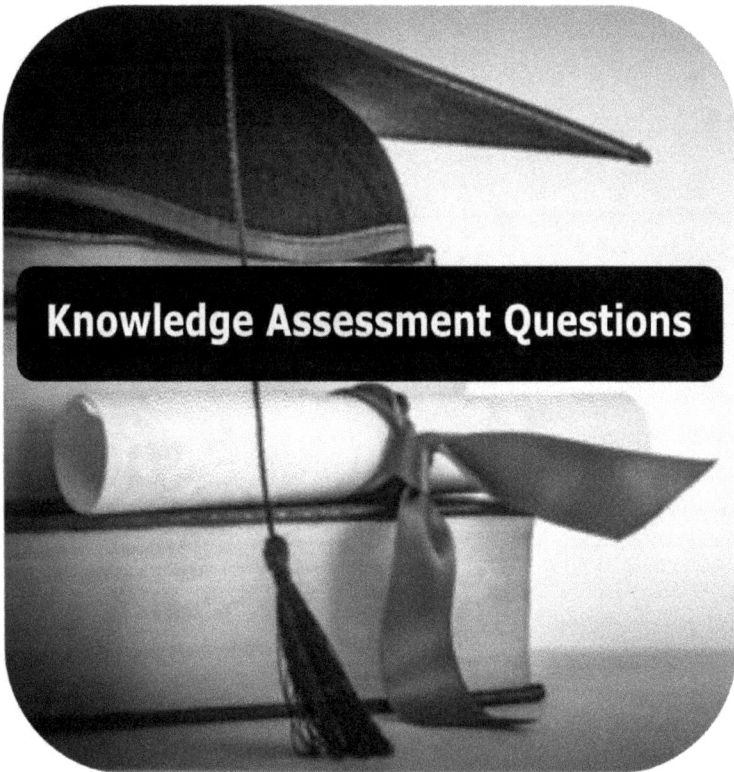

Knowledge Assessment Questions

The following knowledge assessment questions are presented as true / false, multiple choice, and fill-in-the-blank. The correct answers are provided in an Answer Key at the end of the text. These questions may or may not be presented on the actual certification exam.

Domain 12: Knowledge Assessment Questions

1. Which option below is **not** a characteristic or goal of the relationship between Cloud Service Providers and Cloud Customers?

A. Provider: Minimize Service Labor

B. Customer: Maximize Capabilities

C. Customer: Maximize Expenses

D. Contracts and SLA's are Vital

E. None of the Above

2. Some element of _____ exists between the customer and the provider because they have somewhat different goals.

A. Financial Relationship

B. Professional Relationship

C. Contractual Relationship

D. Adversarial Relationship

E. None of the Above

3. Which option below is **not** a characteristic of the shared responsibility between the Cloud Service Provider and the Cloud Customer for Monitoring and Testing management?

A. Established by Formal Agreement in Legal Contracts

B. Increases Risk of Harm and Disclosure

C. Customer Access is Very Limited

D. Occurs in Addition to Provider Efforts

E. None of the Above

4. The cloud provider must apply the proper security controls according to a customers' relevant regulatory frameworks and _____.

A. Confidentiality Agreement

B. Service Contract

C. Planned Usage

D. Geographic Location

E. None of the Above

5. Which option below is **not** a responsibility of the Cloud Service Provider when considering the protection of its physical plant?

A. TPM Standard for BIOS Firmware

B. Managed Hardware Configuration

C. Incident / Forensic / Attribution

D. Configure Secure Remote Access

E. None of the Above

6. In _____ cloud service models, the customer and their users will need to access and modify the data at various levels.

A. IaaS

B. All

C. PaaS

D. SaaS

E. None of the Above

7. Which option below is **not** a characteristic or challenge for the Cloud Customer when considering the lack of allowed access to a Cloud Provider environment?

A. A Beneficial yet Challenging Situation

B. Customer Cannot Verify or Validate Assertions

C. Customer Knowledge = More Risk

D. Decreases Trust in the Cloud Provider

E. None of the Above

8. By reviewing the type of _____ utilized by the cloud customer, the responsibilities can be assigned to the appropriate party.

A. Service Model

B. Virtualization

C. Payment Processing

D. Data Format

E. None of the Above

9. Which option below is **not** a responsibility of the Cloud Service Provider when considering the protection of its secure logical framework?

A. Configuration Policy Enforcement

B. Non-Attenuation of Potential Risks

C. Configure Secure VM Elements

D. Data Leakage / Malicious Aggregation

E. None of the Above

10. The _____ is a large attack surface and offers many potential vectors to malicious actors if not secured correctly.

A. Power System

B. Backup System

C. Email System

D. Operating System

E. None of the Above

11. Which option below is **not** a responsibility of the Cloud Service Provider when considering the protection of its secure networking capability?

A. Conduct Vulnerability Assessments

B. Utilize IDS / IPS Devices

C. Utilize Virtual Private Networks (VPNs)

D. Ensure Use of "Data Encryption Standard" (DES)

E. None of the Above

12. In addition to securing the hardware components the cloud provider must ensure that the _____ are equally protected.

A. Facility Entrances

B. Perimeter Fences

C. Logical Elements

D. Datacenter Facility

E. None of the Above

13. Some element of adversarial relationship exists between the customer and the cloud provider because they have somewhat different goals.

1. True

2. False

14. An area where cloud providers and cloud customers often fail to find common ground in sharing responsibilities is in security monitoring and testing.

1. True

2. False

15. In addition to securing the hardware components, the cloud provider must ensure that the logical framework elements are equally protected.

1. True

2. False

16. The cloud provider will have a limited number of reasons to allow the customer any physical access to the facility containing customer data.

1. True

2. False

17. The cloud provider must apply the proper security controls according to a customers' relevant regulatory frameworks and planned usage.

1. True

2. False

18. The operating system in a cloud environment is a smaller attack surface and offers limited potential vectors to malicious actors if not secured correctly.

1. True

2. False

DOMAIN 13

Legal Considerations in Distributed Cloud Networks

Criminal Law

Criminal law involves all legal matters where the government conflicts with any person, group or entity that violates various statutes. It is enacted by state legislatures and can impose penalties that include fines, imprisonment, or even death. Criminal law applies to state and federal jurisdictions and is adjudicated in various state and federal courts.

States typically handle the prosecution of violations as they have similar criminal laws to the federal system. In those cases in which both federal and state law may be applied in a prosecution, the most stringent laws are the ones typically applied.

Civil Law

Civil law is the body of laws and statutes that deal with personal or community-based law (non-criminal). It is enacted by state legislatures for the purpose of governing private citizens and entities. The implementation of a civil law typically occurs in the form of "lawsuits" or "litigation." Common uses for civil law are breach of contract and adjudication of tort laws (harm resulting from unlawful actions).

Administrative Law

Administrative law is a body of law that affects most people; it is not created by legislatures, but by executive decision and function. Although it impacts the highest majority of people it tends to be the least discussed. Federal agencies representing the Executive Branch of government are the enforcement mechanisms for this category of law. Listed below are five common issues that administrative law typically adjudicates on a regular basis.

1. Intellectual Property Law
2. Copyrights (Expression of Ideas)
3. Trademarks (Brand Identity)
4. Patents (Inventions and Processes)
5. Trade Secrets

International Law

International law determines how to settle disputes and manage relationships between countries and their respective entities. It is an accumulation of conventions establishing rules agreed upon by all signing parties. International law builds its foundation of practiced customs accepted by law, general principles of recognized law in civilized countries, and judicial decisions establishing precedent of law. The interpretation and application of international law will change from country to country based on internal relationships and political conditions. Listed below are three typical circumstances in which international law is applied.

1. Trade Regulations
2. Tariff Structures
3. Treaties (Solve Disputes and Formalize Alliances)

Doctrine of the Proper Law

The *Doctrine of the Proper Law* is a term used to describe the processes associated with determining what legal jurisdiction will hear disputes. Additionally, courts will often refer to *Restatement (Second) Conflict of Laws*, a legal concept that keeps courts aware of current legal precedents and decisions relating to jurisdiction. It is not always a simple matter to determine the jurisdiction in which a case will be heard. For example, consider these geographical complexities regarding a data breach of a major retailer:

1. The Company is Based in the United States
2. Payment Processing is Executed in Canada
3. Customer Goods are Shipped from Singapore
4. Customer Data (PII) is Stored in Ireland

International courts must determine which jurisdiction will hear the case if each entity mentioned above contributed in some way to the breach of customer data. It is a common practice to establish the jurisdiction closest to the area with the largest population of harmed individuals. However, courts may agree to change the venue to a jurisdiction with the most stringent laws.

Relevant U.S. Laws

Stored Communication Act (SCA):

Enacted as part of Title II of the *Electronic Communications Privacy Act* of 1986 (ECPA), the SCA addresses both voluntary and compelled disclosure of stored wire and electronic communications and transactional records held by third parties. The ECPA was designed as an extension of the protections previously offered by the *Computer Fraud and Abuse Act* (CFAA) of 1986.

Health Insurance Portability and Accountability Act (HIPAA):

The federal *Health Insurance Portability and Accountability Act* of 1996 is a set of federal laws governing the handling of *personal health information* (PHI). The *Office of Civil Rights* (OCR) is the enforcement arm of the *Department of Health and Human Services* (DHHS) and oversees audit findings, policy violations, and unreported breaches.

Gramm-Leach-Bliley Act (GLBA):

The *Gramm-Leach-Bliley Act* (GLBA) also known as the *Financial Services Modernization Act* of 1999, was created to allow banks and financial institutions to merge. It requires institutions to have a written information security plan (ISP) and an information security officer (ISO) to implement and manage the ISP.

Sarbanes-Oxley Act (SOX):

The *Sarbanes-Oxley Act* was enacted in 2002 as an attempt to prevent unexpected financial collapse due to fraudulent accounting practices, poor audit practices, inadequate financial controls, and poor oversight by governing boards of directors. The *Securities and Exchange Commission* (SEC is responsible for establishing standards, guidelines, conducting audits, and imposing fines should an aspect of SOX be violated.

EU Data Protection Directive 95/46 EC

The *European Union's Data Protection Directive* of 1995, referred to as the "Data Directive," was the first major EU data privacy law. Unlike the United States—which creates privacy laws and regulations based on industries—the European Union has created privacy laws which are broad, sweeping, and industry agnostic. Enacted by the European Parliament and Council in 1995, this series of laws was fully implemented in 1998.

In an effort to harmonize privacy laws within member states of the EU, the General Data Protection Regulation was enacted in 2016 and made enforceable in 2018. Although GDPR has officially replaced the "Data Directive," the seven foundational principles of EU privacy law listed below have remained the same.

1. **Notice**: Individual Must be Informed
2. **Choice**: Disclosure of PII is Opt-In, not Opt-Out
3. **Purpose**: Informed of Specific Use of PII
4. **Access**: Individual Allowed Copies of PII
5. **Integrity**: Individual can Correct Any Information
6. **Security**: Organizations are Liable for Protecting Any PII
7. **Enforcement**: All PII Entities are Subject to EU Authorities

Safe Harbor

The *Privacy Regulation* (GDPR) supersedes the *Data Directive* and ends the Safe Harbor program, replacing it with a program called "Privacy Shield." The terms of compliance companies handling PII in the EU now face are much more stringent than those originally included in safe harbor. Organizations must agree to auditing and select a federal authority to be responsible for enforcement. An organization may also agree to GDPR terms by including a formal statement of compliance in their corporate charter under the sections of "Binding Corporate Rules" or "Standard Contractual Clauses." The penalties face by US-based companies for non-compliance with GDPR tend to be both assured and severe.

Personal and Data Privacy Issues

Due to the decentralized nature of cloud computing, many geographic disparities may present critical personal and data privacy issues. The focus of these concerns will change from entity to entity based on organizational structure and the geographical location of an individuals' PII. Listed below are six areas of concern BCP managers should take into consideration when assessing the storage of PII in geographically dispersed locations.

1. eDiscovery
2. Chain of Custody
3. Forensic Requirements
4. Direct and Indirect PII Identifiers
5. Contractual and Regulated PII
6. International Conflict Resolution

eDiscovery

Electronic Discovery (eDiscovery) refers to the process of identifying and obtaining evidence for prosecutorial or litigation purposes. Given the centralized nature of cloud computing assets, locating specific records can be challenging. There are many issues to consider when engaged in eDiscovery operations in multitenant environments. Specific customer data must we identified within shared resource—then collected and preserved as evidence—without intruding on third-party data privacy rights. This can be further imapcted by contractual agreements between customers and the cloud service providers.

Chain of Custody

All evidence needs to be tracked and monitored from the time it is recognized as evidence and acquired for that purpose. BCP managers must incorporate the guidance of professional legal counsel in all *chain of custody* matters. Strict guidelines apply to the preservation and integrity of evidence. Only specific and trusted personnel should be involved in the process, and there can be no gaps in the evidence control timeline. Listed below are four questions regarding evidence collection and chain of custody when performing these operations in cloud computing environments.

1. What People had Access to the Evidence?
2. Where Was the Evidence Stored?
3. What Access Controls were in Place?
4. What Modifications and/or was Analysis Done?

Forensic Requirements

Decentralized data and its movement, storage, and processing across geographic boundaries leads to complex challenges for forensics. Although there is demand for an international forensics standard that would be applicable to all parties and at all locations, no such standard exists currently.

In the absence of such a standard imposed by international laws and treaties, a number of established and accepted standards exist to ease the complexity and burden. Listed below are four standards approved by the *International Standard for Organization* (ISO) that are providing effective guidance in geographically dispersed locations.

1. ISO/IEC 27037:2012   (Collection)
2. ISO/IEC 27041:2015   (Incidents)
3. ISO/IEC 27042:2015   (Analysis)
4. ISO/IEC 27050:2016**   (eDiscovery)

** ISO/IEC 27050:2016 is currently the most widely accepted standard within the internal community.

Legal Considerations in Distributed Cloud Networks

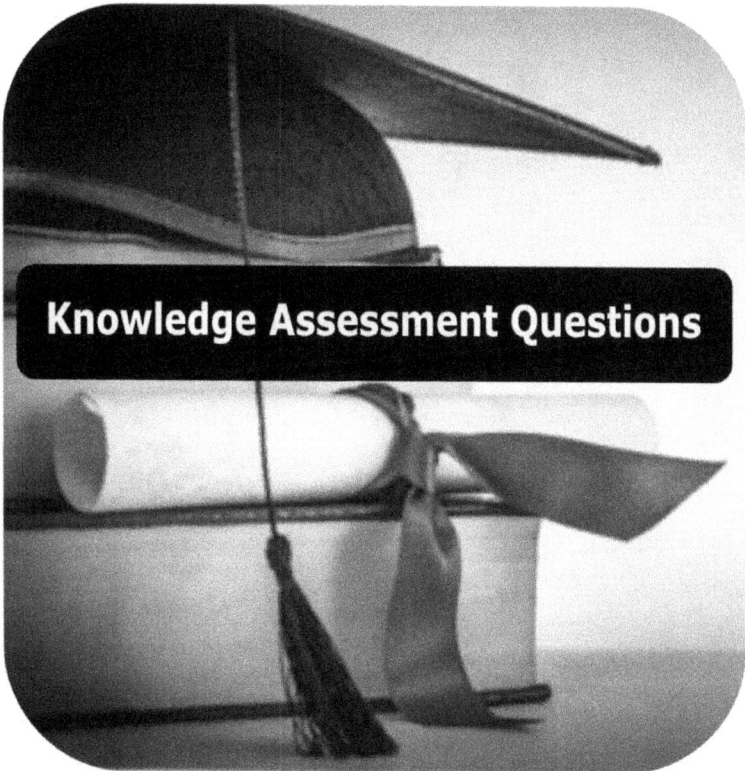

The following knowledge assessment questions are presented as true / false, multiple choice, and fill-in-the-blank. The correct answers are provided in an Answer Key at the end of the text. These questions may or may not be presented on the actual certification exam.

Domain 13: Knowledge Assessment Questions

1. Which option below is **not** a characteristic or goal of Criminal Law?

A. Includes Various Federal and State Courts

B. Penalties Include Fines, Imprisonment or Death

C. The Most Stringent Law Applies

D. Laws Enacted by Federal Agencies

E. None of the Above

2. _____ involves all legal matters where the government conflicts with any person, group or entity that violates various statutes.

A. International Law

B. Administrative Law

C. Civil Law

D. Criminal Law

E. None of the Above

3. Which option below is the most widely accepted standard used for Cloud Computing in an international environment when considering "Forensic Requirement" issues?

A. ISO/IEC 27037:2012 (Collection)

B. ISO/IEC 27041:2015 (Incidents)

C. ISO/IEC 27042:2015 (Analysis)

D. ISO/IEC 27050:2016 (eDiscovery)

E. All of the Above

4. _____ refers to the process of identifying and obtaining evidence for prosecutorial or litigation purposes.

A. Search and Seizure

B. Rules of Evidence

C. eDiscovery

D. Chain of Custody

E. None of the Above

5. Which option below is **not** a characteristic or goal of Civil Law?

A. Law Governs Private Citizens

B. Referred to as "Lawsuits" or "Litigation"

C. Adopted for Private and Public Entities

D. Includes Tort and Contract Law

E. None of the Above

6. _____ is the body of laws and statutes that deal with personal or community-based law.

A. International Law

B. Administrative Law

C. Civil Law

D. Criminal Law

E. None of the Above

7. Which option below is **not** a characteristic or goal of Cloud Computing in an international environment when considering "Chain of Custody" issues?

A. Minimal Gaps in the Control Timeline

B. What Modifications and/or Analysis Done?

C. Specific and Trusted Personnel

D. Where Was the Evidence Stored?

E. None of the Above

8. Due to the _____ nature of cloud computing, many geographic disparities may present critical personal and data privacy issues.

A. Centralized

B. Compartmentalized

C. Expanding

D. Decentralized

E. None of the Above

9. Which option below is **not** a characteristic or goal of Administrative Law?

A. Addresses Intellectual Property Law

B. Enacted by State Legislatures

C. Addresses Patents and Copyrights

D. Addresses Trademarks and Trade Secrets

E. None of the Above

10. _____ is a body of law that affects most people; it is not created by legislatures, but by executive decision and function.

A. International Law

B. Administrative Law

C. Civil Law

D. Criminal Law

E. None of the Above

11. Which option below is **not** a characteristic or goal of Cloud Computing in an international environment when considering "eDiscovery" issues?

A. Not Intruding on Third-Party Data

B. Not Impacted by Contractual Agreements

C. Multitenant Environment Challenges

D. Collection and Preservation of Evidence

E. None of the Above

12. _____ is a term used to describe the processes associated with determining what legal jurisdiction will hear disputes.

A. Doctrine of the Proper Law

B. Doctrine of Correlative Rights

C. Doctrine of Res Judicata

D. Doctrine of Equivalents

E. None of the Above

13. Criminal law involves all legal matters where a business entity conflicts with any person, group or entity that violates various statutes.

1. True

2. False

14. Decentralized data and its movement, storage, and processing across geographic boundaries leads to complex challenges for forensics.

1. True

2. False

15. Administrative law is a body of law that affects most people; it is created by legislatures and enforced by executive decision and function.

1. True

2. False

16. Electronic Discovery (eDiscovery) refers to the process of identifying and obtaining evidence for prosecutorial or litigation purposes.

1. True

2. False

17. Intercontinental law determines how to settle disputes and manage relationships between countries and their respective entities.

1. True

2. False

18. The Privacy Regulation supersedes the Data Directive and ends the Safe Harbor program, replacing it with a program called Privacy Shield.

1. True

2. False

Regulation and Compliance in Cloud Computing

Diverse Geographical Locations

A great deal of the difficulty in managing the legal aspects of cloud computing stems from the design of the cloud assets themselves. Cloud assets are dispersed and distributed by necessity, and these assets are being allocated and re-allocated continually making them difficult to identify and control. The jurisdictions in which the assets are allocated tend to have unique governance, and the legislation within a given jurisdiction is always in flux. Finally, the vagaries of law that are created when technology outpaces the ability of legislatures typically creates slow policy responses.

Organizational Cloud Policies

Policies are a foundational element of organizational governance and risk management programs, and ensure companies operate within their risk profiles. Key stakeholders are usually not directly involved in the creation of organizational policies, but their perceptions can have a dramatic influence on the risk acceptance that leads to the formation of policy. The creation of policies will change from entity to entity based on organizational structure and a regulatory environment that can limit risk appetite. Listed below are four key stakeholders that typically have the most impact on the creation of cloud computing policies.

1. Board of Directors
2. Senior Leadership
3. Investors and Stakeholders
4. Regulatory and Compliance Entities

Engaging Stakeholders

Identifying and engaging relevant stakeholders is vital to the success of any cloud computing discussions, programs, or projects. Malleable policies should always exist to reflect changes in the organization, but this is especially true when considering the issue of migrating data to the cloud. Cloud risks and benefits are different from their legacy counterparts. For this reason, new policies must be created, and existing policies must be revisited often.

Prioritizing Jurisdictions

The variety and vagaries of multijurisdictional law make the regulatory stakeholders and their input complicated for cloud services. The cloud customers' jurisdiction is earth, making it impossible to craft policy for individual jurisdictions. Additionally, each of these jurisdictions are inherently in conflict (federal vs. state vs. county vs. city vs. the international market). The criteria for prioritizing jurisdictions will change from entity to entity based on organizational structure and geographical location. Listed below are three considerations when choosing a jurisdiction from which organizational policy will be based.

1. Largest Residence of the Providers' End Clientele
2. Location of Most of the Cloud Functionality
3. Jurisdiction with the Most Bearing on Organizational Policy

Communicating Policy

Once a cloud computing policy has been formally accepted, it must be published and disseminated among those affected by the policy. In the best of times, organizational communication is challenging; the issue of cloud computing is increasing that complexity. Providers may be dealing with thousands of customers, and the IT staff of the organization may not be local.

Despite this, the internal and external stakeholders should be kept abreast of any changes or issues related to policies and operations. The methods by which organizations communicate policies will change from entity to entity based on organizational structure stakeholder needs. Listed below are seven categories of key stakeholders that must always be kept informed.

1. Information Technology and Information Security
2. Human Resource Management
3. Vendor and Client Management
4. Compliance and Regulatory Entities
5. Risk Management and Security Management
6. Finance and Accounting Management
7. Operational Management

Policy Communication Challenges

When discussing these matters with stakeholders, remember they will most likely not have a complete grasp of cloud computing technology. That fact makes it even more crucial for the BCP manager to communicate messages regarding policy clearly and concisely. Good communication will allow senior leadership and key stakeholders to make factual decisions. Poor communication will create confusion and lead to hearsay. Listed below are five common challenges to communicating policy for BCP managers in organizations with dispersed geographical locations.

1. A Disparate Administrative Workforce
2. Time Zone and Language Differences
3. Ignorance of Cloud Concepts and Models
4. Poor Understanding of Business Drivers
5. Poor Understanding of Risk Appetite

The Cloud in Enterprise Risk Management

It is vitally important that both the cloud customer and the cloud provider focus on risk management and the challenges of cloud computing. The assessment methods and responses to risk will change from entity to entity based on organizational structure and context. Listed below are the five options an organization has when considering how potential risk will be addressed.

1. Risk Avoidance   (Ignore the Problem)
2. Risk Avoidance   (Reject the Risk Scenario)
3. Risk Acceptance   (Within Risk Appetite Level)
4. Risk Transference   (Insurance and Third Parties)
5. Risk Mitigation   (Never Eliminated Completely)

Risk Management Frameworks: ISO 31000:2009

The *ISO 31000:2009* is an international standard focused on creating, implementing, and reviewing risk management practices and processes. The adoption of this framework will change from entity to entity based on organizational structure and geographical location. Listed below are seven characteristics of ISO 31000:2009 with which the BCP manager should become familiar before adoption into a risk management program.

1. Integrate Organizational Procedures
2. Engage in Decision-Making Process
3. Explicitly Address Uncertainty
4. Based on Best Available Information
5. Consider Human and Cultural Factors
6. The Program Must be Transparent and Inclusive
7. The Program Must be Dynamic, Iterative, and Responsive

Risk Management Frameworks: NIST SP 800-39

This risk management framework is a methodology for handling all risk in a holistic, comprehensive, and continual manner. It has now superseded the older "Certification and Accreditation" model that was heavily relied upon by federal agencies in the United States. Although this is an excellent model for domestic operations it is not formally accepted in international markets. This is a crucial fact as some international markets will exclude organizations that are not aligned with ISO standards. Listed below are four characteristics of *NIST SP 800-39* with which the BCP manager should become familiar before adoption into a risk management program.

1. The Framework Relies Heavily on Automation
2. Foundational Purpose is Risk Analysis and Assessment
3. Advocates Assessment-Based Security Controls
4. Advocates Continuous Monitoring and Improvement

Risk Management Frameworks: ENISA

The *European Union Agency for Network and Information Security* (ENISA) is international within Europe, but not globally accepted like ISO standards. It is a comprehensive framework which identifies 35 types of common risks to information systems, and specifically identifies eight security risks based on likelihood. Listed below are the top five specific risks of the eight identified by ENISA with which the BCP manager should become familiar before adoption into a risk management program.

Domain 14: *Regulation and Compliance in Cloud Computing*

1. Loss of Program Governance
2. Vendor Lock-In
3. Management Interface Failure
4. Malicious Internal Threats
5. Incomplete and/or Insecure Data Deletion

Risk Management Metrics

To understand whether control mechanisms and policies are effective, it is important to identify metrics that accurately reflect the risk management program. Levels of risk must be defined and described—quantitatively and qualitatively—and metrics must be attached to the specific risks identified. The levels used to describe risk will change from entity to entity based on organizational structure and context. Listed below are the five levels of risk that are common to most risk management programs.

1. Critical   (Red)
2. High   (Orange)
3. Moderate   (Yellow)
4. Low   (Blue)
5. Minimal   (Green)

Contracts and Service-Level Agreements

The most important documents establishing, defining, and enforcing the relationship between the cloud customer and the provider are contracts and service level agreements (SLA's). The terms tend to be used interchangeably but they are distinct and different documents. An important relationship exists between both documents in that they support and corroborate each other. Listed below are six key characteristics and differences between a contract and an SLA with which the BCP manager should become familiar before accepting the task of reviewing these types of documents.

1. **Contract**: Describes Mutual Responsibilities
2. **Contract**: Defines Services to be Offered

3. **Contract**: Defines Security Provisions to be Provided
4. **Contract**: Stipulates Penalties for Breach of Contract
5. **SLA**: Defines Performance-Based Numerical Metrics
6. **SLA**: Used as a Measurement for Contract Terms

Service-Level Agreements

While both the contract and SLA may contain numerical values, the SLA will expressly include metrics to determine if contractual goals are met. It is important that the cloud customer consider all possible situations and risks associated with cloud business processes and requirements, as this will have a significant impact on negotiating the SLA with the cloud provider.

The metrics included in an SLA to be measured will change from entity to entity based on organizational structure and need. Listed below are 12 common metrics typically included in SLA's for measurement which the BCP manager should become familiar before accepting the task of reviewing this of document.

1. Availability Metrics
2. Outage Duration Metrics
3. Capacity Metrics
4. Performance Metrics
5. Storage Device Metrics
6. Server Capacity Metrics
7. Instance Start-Up Time Metrics
8. Response Time Metrics
9. Completion Time Metrics
10. Mean Time to Switchover Metrics
11. Logging and Reporting Metrics
12. Server Scalability Metrics

DOMAIN 14

Regulation and Compliance in Cloud Computing

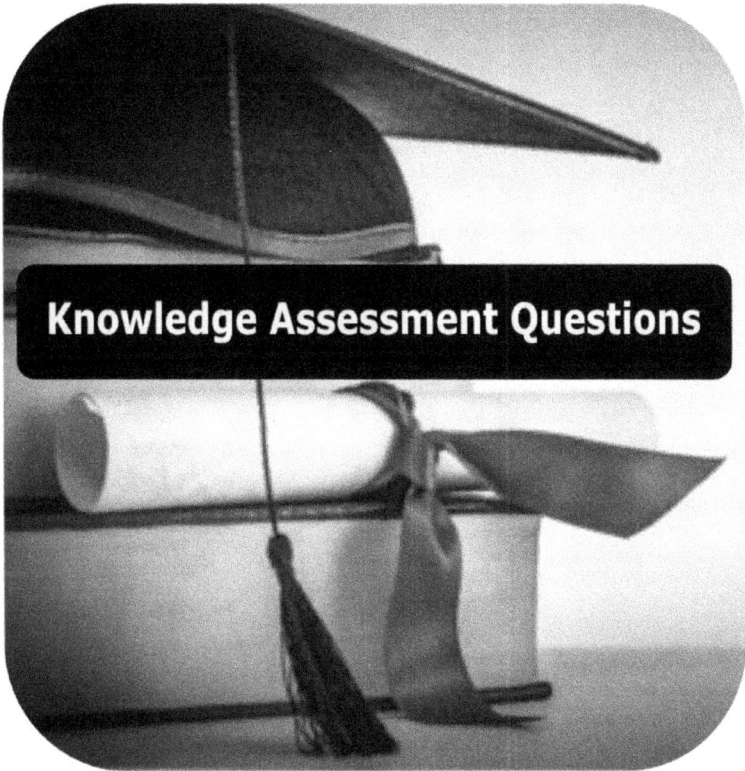

Knowledge Assessment Questions

The following knowledge assessment questions are presented as true / false, multiple choice, and fill-in-the-blank. The correct answers are provided in an Answer Key at the end of the text. These questions may or may not be presented on the actual certification exam.

Domain 14: Knowledge Assessment Questions

1. Which option below is **not** a characteristic or concern of Cloud Computing when considering data security in diverse geographic locations?

A. Jurisdictions with Similar Governance

B. Data is Dispersed by Necessity

C. Resources Constantly Re-Allocated

D. Legislation is Always in Flux

E. None of the Above

2. A great deal of the difficulty in managing the legal aspects of cloud computing stems from the _____ of the cloud assets themselves.

A. Location

B. Design

C. Costs

D. Management

E. None of the Above

3. Which option below is **not** a metric intended to be measured by a Service Level Agreement (SLA)?

A. Financial Metrics

B. Availability Metrics

C. Performance Metrics

D. Capacity Metrics

E. None of the Above

4. The _____ risk management framework is a methodology for handling all risk in a holistic, comprehensive, and continual manner.

A. ISO 31000:2009

B. Service Contract

C. NIST SP 800-37

D. ENISA

E. None of the Above

5. Which option below is **not** a characteristic or concern when considering the creation of organizational policies in Cloud environments?

A. Perceptions can Influence Risk Acceptance

B. Regulation Can Increase Risk Appetite

C. Stakeholders are Not Directly Involved

D. Influence of Senior Leadership

E. None of the Above

6. _____ are a foundational element of governance and risk management programs and ensure companies operate within their risk profiles.

A. Frameworks

B. Guidelines

C. Policies

D. Standards

E. None of the Above

7. Which option below is **not** a characteristic or function of a Service Contract or its attached Service Level Agreement (SLA)?

A. Contract: Describes Responsibilities

B. SLA: Defines Numerical Metrics

C. Contract: Services Offered

D. SLA: Stipulates Penalties

E. None of the Above

8. While both the service contracts and SLA may contain numerical values, the _____ will expressly include metrics to determine if contractual goals are met.

A. Contract Amendments

B. Service Contract

C. Statement of Work

D. Service Level Agreement

E. None of the Above

9. Which option below is **not** a characteristic or concern when engaging stakeholders as an organization considers a migration to a cloud environment?

A. Cloud Risks and Benefits are Different

B. Policies Reflect Organizational Changes

C. Existing Policies Cannot be Malleable

D. Policies Must be Revisited Often

E. None of the Above

10. The variety and vagaries of _____ law make the regulatory stakeholders and their input complicated for cloud services.

A. Contractual

B. Administrative

C. Regulatory

D. Multijurisdictional

E. None of the Above

11. Which option below is **not** a characteristic or goal of the European Union Agency for Network and Information Security Risk Management Framework?

A. Identifies 35 Types of Risks

B. Lists 8 Security Risks Based on Likelihood

C. Concerned about Management Interface Failure

D. Concerned about Complete / Secure Data Deletion

E. None of the Above

12. It is vitally important that both the customer and the cloud provider focus on _____ and the challenges of cloud computing.

A. Risk Management

B. Service Level Agreements

C. Nondisclosure Agreements

D. Certification

E. None of the Above

13. A great deal of the difficulty in managing the legal aspects of cloud computing stems from the design of the cloud policies and procedures.

1. True

2. False

14. It is important that the cloud customer consider all possible situations and risks associated with cloud business processes and requirements when signing Service Level Agreements (SLAs).

1. True

2. False

15. Identifying and engaging relevant business models is vital to the success of any cloud computing discussions, programs, or projects.

1. True

2. False

16. The most important documents establishing, defining, and enforcing the relationship between the customer and provider are contracts and Service Level Agreements (SLAs).

1. True

2. False

17. Once a policy has been formally accepted, it must be approved by the Board of Directors and added to the Business Continuity Plan (BCP).

1. True

2. False

18. The European Union Agency for Network and Information Security (ENISA) is international within Europe, but not globally accepted like ISO.

1. True

2. False

Understanding the Structure of Legal Contracts

*** Legal Advice Disclaimer ***

The information provided in this course does not, and is not intended to, constitute legal advice; all information is for general informational and educational purposes only. Google is a useful tool for researching legal issues, but Google did **not** pass any states' bar exam. If you have questions regarding advanced topics in technology, always consult a technology expert. If you have questions regarding legal issues, always consult legal counsel. This content has been created to provide BCP managers with a general understanding of review contracts and service level agreements. However, general understanding is not equivalent to expertise.

Good Fences Make Good Neighbors

The best way to avoid arguments in a business relationship is to write down the parties' expectations ahead of time. Contracts become a boundary marker (like a fence) that explain where the responsibilities of the parties begin and end. Contracts are not designed for the purpose winning lawsuits later, nor are they a result of a lack of trust between the parties. Negotiating contracts can reveal mismatched expectations and sort out details prior to formalizing a relationship. Good contracts attempt to prevent disputes and keep the involved parties out of court.

"Legalese" Does Not Exist

Contrary to widely held belief, there is no such things as "legalese," just as there is no "technolese" or "medicalese." Contracts and attorneys may use specialized industry shorthand to convey thought (i.e., *pro forma* or *prima facie*), but so do those in the IT field (*bot*, *dongle*, or *ping*) and it is accepted without a second thought. Even though some attorneys feel the need to use stilted language and long sentences, most modern contracts are written in plain language both parties can understand. When encountering an unknown legal term, use *Black's Law Dictionary* as a reference or seek out someone with legal expertise. When encountering long sentences that seem to never end, just relax, and read slowly.

Seek Best Options Over "Fairness"

Each party negotiating a business relationship has a choice about whether to enter a contract; neither side owes the other any special considerations or terms. Many individuals believe contracts should be "fair," but it is impossible to define the word in legal terms. Is voluntarily accepting bad terms unfair, and if the majority accepts those terms, are the terms unfair at all? Focusing on "fair" may cause and individual reviewing a contract to reject terms that make economic sense or accept terms that are ridiculous or absurd. Instead of focusing of "fair," focus on leverage as the guiding principle during contract negotiations and seek the best possible outcome for the relationship.

General Contract Structures

Information Technology contracts can be organized into three groups: *prime clauses, general clauses*, and *boilerplate clauses*. Listed below are the five basic components commonly used in the structure of legal contracts.

1. Introduction and Recitals
2. Definitions
3. Prime Clauses
4. General Clauses
5. Boilerplate Clauses

Prime Clauses

Customers should protect themselves against unclear descriptions and ensure all promises address the expectation of help needed. Listed below are six examples of common issues a BCP manager may expect to review in prime clauses of contracts.

1. Defining the Professional Service
2. Statements of Work (Separate)
3. Change Order Procedures
4. Customer Fees
5. Distributor and Reseller Fees
6. Due Dates and Invoices

General Causes

The term "General Clauses" is a catch-all category that refers to issues not addressed in a primary or boilerplate clause. The one characteristic shared by all elements of general clauses is that they generate the most disagreement, debate, and compromise between the parties involved in the contract negotiation. Listed below are 14 examples of common issues a BCP manager may expect to review in general clauses of contracts.

1. Technical Specifications
2. Service Level Agreements
3. Response, Repair, and Remedy
4. Maintenance, Upgrades, and Updates
5. Schedules and Milestones
6. Delivery, Acceptance, and Rejection
7. Nondisclosure and Confidentiality
8. Data Management and Security
9. General and Specific Indemnity
10. Limitation of Liability
11. Non-Compete and Non-Solicit Stipulations
12. Financial Stability and Reporting
13. Alternative Dispute Resolution
14. Term and Termination of the Contract

Boilerplate Clauses

The boilerplate clauses include a set of terms usually placed at the end of a contract and used for introductory material as well. One cannot predict what issues may arise in a business relationship, so one cannot know when boilerplate clauses will become vital. Listed below are 14 examples of common issues a BCP manager may expect to review in general clauses of contracts.

1. Introductions and Recitals
2. Definitions (Terms Used Often in the Contract)
3. Time Is of the Essence (Time/Breach Clause)
4. Use of Independent Contractors
5. Choice of Law and Courts
6. Government Restricted Rights
7. Technology Export Requirements (International Clients)

8. Force Majeure ("Acts of God" and List of Specific Events)
9. Severability (Limits Unknown Impact of Events)
10. Bankruptcy Rights
11. Conflicts Among Attachments
12. Construction (How Unclear Terms are Defined in Courts)
13. Entire Agreement (no Prior Documents)
14. Amendments (Typical and Unilateral)

SLA and Contract Review Process

Most lawsuits arise from contracts that are not clear, complete, and that do not express the agreement as it was understood by the parties. Listed below are five common guidelines a BCP manager should follow when reviewing contracts and Service Level Agreements.

1. Agree on all Definitions
2. Make no Assumptions (Get Clarification)
3. Identify Missing Items (Omissions)
4. Feel Comfortable Changing the Boilerplate as Needed
5. Always Seek a Second Opinion for Reviews

General Contract Review Checklist

When reviewing contracts and service level agreements, consider the use of checklists to help ensure a consistent approach. The checklists items listed below are not all-inclusive and are only offered as a minimal example of contract review considerations.

1. Ensure all Parties are Properly Identified
2. Ensure all Capitalized Terms are Defined
3. Ensure all Signature and Initial Blocks Correct
4. Ensure all Referenced Exhibits are Correct and Attached
5. Ensure all Boilerplate is Relevant (Cut and Paste Mistakes)
6. Ensure all Performance Obligations are Accurate
7. Ensure all Payment Terms are Accurate
8. Ensure all Payment Dates and Methods are Accurate
9. Ensure the Service Term and Termination is Correct
10. Ensure the Law, Jurisdiction, and Venue are Correct

Understanding the Structure of Legal Contracts

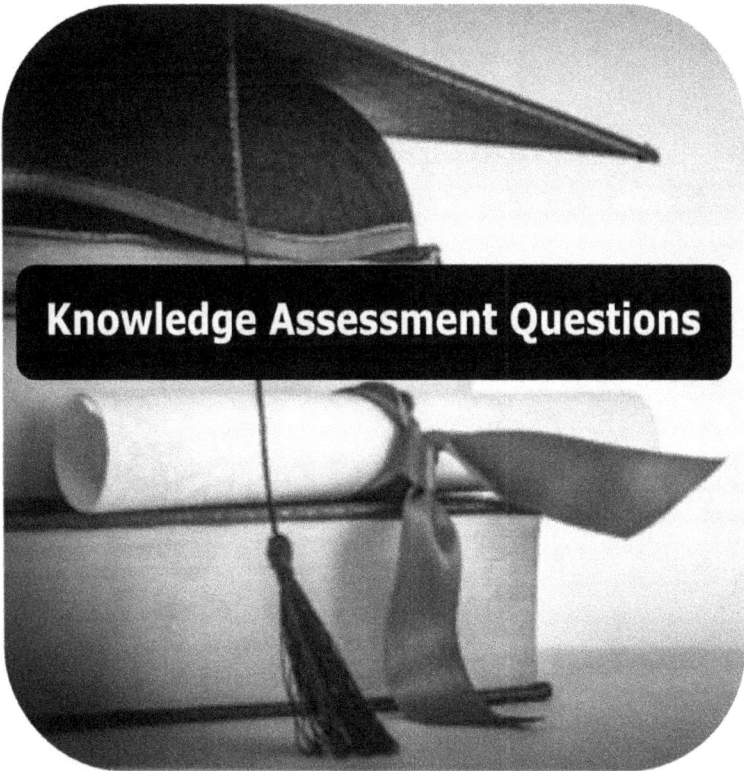

The following knowledge assessment questions are presented as true / false, multiple choice, and fill-in-the-blank. The correct answers are provided in an Answer Key at the end of the text. These questions may or may not be presented on the actual certification exam.

Domain 15: Knowledge Assessment Questions

1. Which option below is **not** a reason why parties engaged in a business venture would choose to utilize a formal contract?

A. Good Contracts Win Disputes

B. Contract Becomes a Boundary Marker

C. Explains Responsibilities of Parties

D. Uncovers Mismatched Expectations

E. None of the Above

2. When reviewing contracts and service level agreements, consider the use of _____ to help ensure a consistent approach.

A. Templates

B. Legal Counsel

C. Co-Workers

D. Checklists

E. None of the Above

3. Which choice below is **not** a component to be taken under consideration when drafting a general contract review checklist?

A. All Capitalized Terms Defined

B. All Exhibits Correct and Attached

C. Law, Jurisdiction, and Venue are Correct

D. All Performance Obligations are Accurate

E. None of the Above

4. IT contract and service level agreement terms can be organized into three groups: Prime Clauses, General Clauses, and _____.

A. Service Level Agreements

B. Statements of Work

C. Boilerplate Clauses

D. Introductions and Recitals

E. None of the Above

5. Which choice below is **not** a reason why choosing the best possible option over "fairness" during contract negotiations is the correct strategy?

A. Impossible to Define "Fair" in Law

B. May Reject Ridiculous Offers

C. Accepting Bad Terms ≠ Unfair

D. May Reject Economic Common Sense

E. None of the Above

6. Most lawsuits arise from contracts that are not clear, complete, and that do not express the agreement as it was _____ by the parties.

A. Intended

B. Written

C. Understood

D. Negotiated

E. None of the Above

7. Which choice below is **not** a function and purpose of a Boilerplate Clause in a formal legal contract?

A. Introductions and Recitals

B. General and Specific Indemnity

C. Force Majeure (Acts of God)

D. Conflicts Among Attachments

E. None of the Above

8. Customers should protect themselves against _____ and ensure all promises address the expectation of help needed.

A. Liability Clauses

B. Opposing Counsel

C. Professional Negotiators

D. Unclear Descriptions

E. None of the Above

9. Which choice below is **not** one of the five standard components of a formal legal contract?

A. Introduction and Recitals

B. Prime Clauses

C. Secondary Clauses

D. Boilerplate Clauses

E. None of the Above

10. You cannot predict what issues may arise in a business relationship, so you cannot know when _____ will become vital.

A. Prime Clauses

B. Boilerplate Clauses

C. General Clauses

D. Contractual Amendments

E. None of the Above

11. Which choice below is **not** a function and purpose of a General Clause in a formal legal contract?

A. Choice of Law and Courts

B. Delivery, Acceptance, and Rejection

C. Schedules and Milestones

D. Response, Repair, and Remedy

E. None of the Above

12. The one characteristic shared by all elements of _____ is that they generate the most disagreement, debate, and compromise.

A. General Clauses

B. Boilerplate Clauses

C. Prime Clauses

D. Contractual Amendments

E. None of the Above

13. The best way to avoid arguments in a business relationship is to write down the parties' expectations ahead of time.

1. True

2. False

14. When reviewing contracts and Service Level Agreements, consider the use of committees and teams to help ensure a consistent approach.

1. True

2. False

15. Each party has a choice about whether to enter into a contract; neither side owes the other any special considerations or terms.

1. True

2. False

16. You cannot predict what issues may arise in a business relationship, so you cannot know when "Boilerplate Clauses" will need to be included in the contract.

1. True

2. False

17. Customers should protect themselves against unclear descriptions in contracts and ensure all promises address the expectation of help needed.

1. True

2. False

18. The one characteristic shared by General Clauses in contracts is that they are the easiest to understand and warrant the least amount of attention.

1. True

2. False

DOMAIN 16

Reviewing Contracts and Service Level Agreements

*** Legal Advice Disclaimer ***

The information provided in this course does not, and is not intended to, constitute legal advice; all information is for general informational and educational purposes only. Google is a useful tool for researching legal issues, but Google did **not** pass any states' bar exam. If you have questions regarding advanced topics in technology, always consult a technology expert. If you have questions regarding legal issues, always consult legal counsel. This content has been created to provide BCP managers with a general understanding of review contracts and service level agreements. However, general understanding is not equivalent to expertise.

Provisions of an Enforceable Contract

A legal contract cannot violate the law in any manner and can become void if either party acts in an illegal fashion. The content of legal contracts will change from entity to entity based on organizational negotiations and legal needs. Listed below are seven common provisions found in all legal contracts.

1. Capacity (Authorized to Enter Contract)
2. Offer
3. Acceptance
4. Competent Parties
5. Mutuality of Obligation
6. Consideration (Time to Consider Terms)
7. Agreement (Both Parties)

MYTH: Guaranteed Uptime = Guaranteed Uptime

There are many commonly held myths and misunderstandings regarding contracts and service level agreements. Once of these misunderstandings can result from contract language defining "guaranteed uptime" of the cloud service. Most providers claim to be operational 99.999% (The Five 9's) of the time, but downtime can mean more than just inaccessible service. The BCP manager must ensure the true meaning of words, and spot caveats to the conditions which will have a negative impact on the organization. Even when the contract between the customer and provider stipulates subpar performance refunds, those refunds rarely cover the tangible losses experienced by the customer. Listed below are four potential areas of impact a BCP manager should consider when reviewing "guaranteed uptime" performance clauses.

1. **Unreliable or Unusable Service**: The providers' service may be functional, but if it is not functioning at a level useful to the customer it does not mean much. Connectivity to the customer is unreliable or unusable, it might as well be considered downtime.

2. **Service Performance Degradation**: Accessing functions with adequate bandwidth will not provide the customer much value if the function is faulty and there is little or no support to be found to remedy the situation quickly.

3. **Scheduled Maintenance Excluded**: In many contracts, guaranteed uptime does not take into consideration scheduled maintenance (guaranteed downtime). The customer must ensure this issue is addressed contractually.

4. **Iterative Maintenance Plans**: Most major cloud service providers use iterative maintenance plans: incremental maintenance plans rotated across the providers' system. However, this is not guaranteed, and the customer must ensure interactive maintenance plans are in the contract.

MYTH: Contracts will Scale with the Business

This is a common misunderstanding between cloud customers and the providers that can have serious impacts on the organization, but which is easily remedied. The service contract and SLA are designed to meet the need of the organization at the time they are negotiated and signed, and they do not typically take any future expansion or contraction into consideration. Organizations can change in size dramatically for a variety of reasons in a short amount of time, and service contracts must take this into consideration. Listed below are five strategies a BCP manager can use to ensure the cloud service contract keeps pace with the needs of the organization.

Domain 16: *Reviewing Contracts and Service Level Agreements*

1. Outline Contract Review Intervals
2. Provider Notification if Customer is Close to Breach
3. Provider Notification if Customers' Service is Underutilized
4. Agreement Negotiations will Begin when Scale Changes
5. Ensure SLA Meetings will Occur "Off Paper" (in Person)

MYTH: Changing Service Providers is Easy

The costs for a customer to change cloud providers can be cost prohibitive and fraught will challenges. A transition clause should be included in the "Term and Termination" section of the cloud contract to avoid overlapping transition costs for the customer, and costly lawsuits for the provider. The transition clause should activate at the time of the contract breach.

For example, if the customer is allocated "X" amount of data to be transferred each month in a yearly contract, and the provider breaches the contract in month 11 causing the customer to transfer data out to a new provider, will that customer be required to pay "11 x X" for the transfer? Issues such as these must be addressed during the contract negotiations.

MYTH: Providers Should Choose Measurements

It is the organizations' responsibility, not the provider, to determine what performance metrics will be measured in service level agreements tied to cloud service contracts. Most providers are inclined to request measurements in their strongest performance areas, while at the same time not revealing their shortcomings to customers. Listed below are five guidelines a BCP manager can use to ensure the proper data is being measured accurately.

1. Decide the Important Metrics for the Company
2. Set Measurable and Specific Benchmarks
3. Avoid Ambiguous Language and/or Numbers
4. Require Monitoring Tools and Timely Reports
5. Demand and Enforce Penalties for Breach of Performance

Contract Negotiation Strategies

Negotiators understand the importance of reaching a win-win solution; when both sides are satisfied, better partnerships are the result. The BCP managers' involvement with contract negotiation will change from entity to entity based on organizational structure and need. Listed below are five proven strategies that should be considered when negotiating cloud service contracts and service level agreements.

1. Make Multiple Offers Simultaneously
2. Include a Matching Right
3. Attempt a Contingency Agreement
4. Negotiate Damages Early in the Process
5. Search for Post-Settlement Settlements

Make Multiple Offers Simultaneously

In negotiations involving many issues, BCP managers can create a great deal of value by making *multiple equivalent simultaneous offers* (MESO). The process begins by identifying several related proposals that are valued equally and presenting the proposals as offers simultaneously. Listed below are three potential benefits of incorporating this action into a negotiation strategy.

1. It Gives Appearance of Flexibility
2. It Increases the Odds of Agreement
3. It may Help to Identify the Oppositions' Preferences

Include a Matching Right

In negotiation strategy, the inclusion of a *matching right* into a contract offer is a guarantee that one side can match any offer that the other side later receives. This option is gaining popularity in contracts at all levels within a wide variety of industries. For example, if a real estate owner leases office space to a customer for one year and then raises the cost of the rent when the lease expires, the current customer has the right to continue the lease at the higher rate before it can be offered to another tenant.

The grantor (provider) must guarantee this right to the holder (customer) by means of legal contract. This arrangement is also commonly referred to as "Right of First Refusal." Listed below are two potential benefits of incorporating this action into a negotiation strategy for a legal contract.

    1. This Right Preserves Mutual Flexibility
    2. It Gives the Flexibility to Match Third-Party Offers

Attempt a Contingent Agreement

In negotiation, parties often reach an impasse because they have different beliefs about the likelihood of future events. In this scenario, "Side A" believes a proposal to be reasonable while "Side B" believe the premise upon which the proposal is founded to be unrealistic.

If parties involved in contract negotiations cannot align on potential outcomes in the future, there is little chance for any agreement in the present. Listed below are four potential benefits of incorporating this action into a negotiation strategy for a legal contract.

    1. Contingent Agreements Are Flexible
    2. "If - Then" Challenges are Easier to Overcome
    3. Talks can Continue Despite Disagreement
    4. Provides an Excellent for Incentives and/or Penalties

Negotiate Damages Early in Process

When formulating the initial contract, the organization can—and should—specify what will happen if any side violates the contract. No matter how well contracts are drafted, lawsuits cause both sides to lose focus on their primary operation. Negotiating damages allows both parties to stipulate the actual cost of a breach to the organizations involved (quantitative losses) as opposed to varying perceptions of the cost (qualitative losses). Organizations (and their negotiators) may not feel comfortable leading with this topic but this benefits both parties.

Domain 16: *Reviewing Contracts and Service Level Agreements*

Listed below are three potential benefits of incorporating this action into a negotiation strategy for a legal contract.

1. Addresses Considerations for Alternate Dispute Resolution
2. Addresses Alternative Means of Compensation
3. Adds a New Issue to the Negotiation (Bargaining Chip)

Search for Post-Settlement Settlements

According to conventional doctrine, the conversation should end once a contract is negotiated for fear of derailing the agreement. That conventional wisdom may not always be practical. Once the contract has been executed there is no harm in testing the other party's willingness to revisit the terms to determine if the existing contract can be improved. There is no pressure for either side to engage in this type of dialogue.

New stipulations and provisions must benefit both parties equally, and either side is free to reject the revised contract if they are so inclined. Listed below are two potential benefits of incorporating this action into a post-negotiation strategy for a legal contract.

1. It can Identify and Create New Sources of Value
2. It can Lead to Increased Mutual Trust Between Parties

DOMAIN 16

Reviewing Contracts and Service Level Agreements

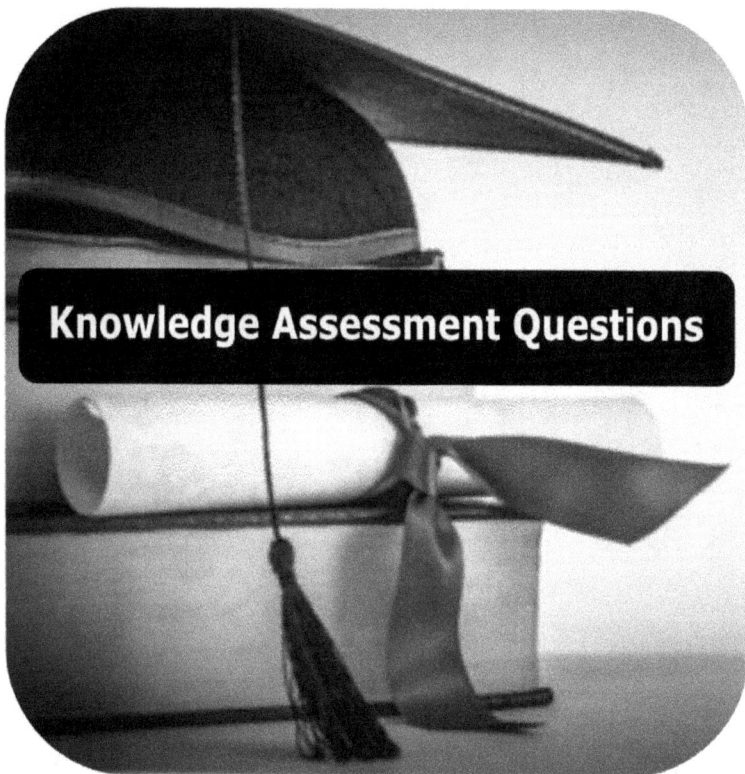

Knowledge Assessment Questions

The following knowledge assessment questions are presented as true / false, multiple choice, and fill-in-the-blank. The correct answers are provided in an Answer Key at the end of the text. These questions may or may not be presented on the actual certification exam.

Domain 16: Knowledge Assessment Questions

1. Which option below is **not** a provision of an enforceable contract?

A. Capacity (Authorized)

B. Competent Parties

C. Mutuality of Obligation

D. Non-Agreement

E. None of the Above

2. In negotiation, parties often reach impasse because they have different beliefs about the likelihood of _____.

A. Service Penalties

B. Breach of Contract

C. Expensive Litigation

D. Future Events

E. None of the Above

3. Which option below is **not** a characteristic of the negotiation strategy of attempting to search for post-settlement settlements?

A. Must Benefit Both Parties Equally

B. Can Create New Sources of Value

C. See if Contract Can be Terminated

D. Can Lead to Increased Mutual Trust

E. None of the Above

4. Negotiators understand the importance of reaching a(n) _____ solution; when both sides are satisfied, better partnerships are the result.

A. Advantageous

B. Zero-Sum Game

C. Win-Win

D. Profitable

E. None of the Above

5. When a Service Level Agreement (SLA) has a "guaranteed uptime" requirement, which option listed below would **not** be a reason to explore that requirement in further detail?

A. Downtime Means More Than "Inaccessible"

B. Scheduled Maintenance Excluded

C. Downtime Refunds > Actual Losses

D. Service Performance Degradation

E. None of the Above

6. In negotiation, include a _____ in your contract; a guarantee that one side can match any offer that the other side later receives.

A. Contingency Agreement

B. Settlement

C. Matching Right

D. Benefit

E. None of the Above

7. Which option below is **not** a characteristic of the negotiation strategy of attempting to negotiate damages early in the process?

A. Stipulate the Cost of the Breach

B. Consider Alternate Dispute Resolution

C. Alternative Means of Compensation

D. Removes a New Issue in the Negotiation

E. None of the Above

8. When formulating the _____ contract you can, and should, specify what will happen if one side violates the contract.

A. Business

B. Technical

C. Operational

D. Initial

E. None of the Above

9. Which option below is **not** a reason why parties engaged in a business contract must ensure the Service Level Agreement (SLA) scales with the business over time?

A. SLA Meets Need at the Time of Negotiation

B. Businesses Do Not Change in Size Dramatically

C. Notification if Service is Underutilized

D. Outline the Contract Review Time Intervals

E. None of the Above

10. A(n) _____ cannot violate the law in any manner and can become void if either party acts in an illegal fashion.

A. Agreement

B. Contract

C. Offer

D. Negotiation

E. None of the Above

11. Which option below is **not** a characteristic of the negotiation strategy of attempting to make a contingency agreement?

A. Talks Postponed During the Disagreement

B. Contingent Agreements Are Flexible

C. Negotiating "if, then" Challenges

D. Excellent for Incentives and Penalties

E. None of the Above

12. A conversation should not end once a contract has been negotiated as either party to the contract may benefit from a potential _____.

A. Post-Settlement Settlement

B. Contingency Agreement

C. Favorable Amendments

D. Matching Right

E. None of the Above

13. A contract cannot violate the state law in which it was written and can become void if both parties to the contract act in an illegal fashion.

1. True

2. False

14. In negotiations, parties often reach an impasse because they have different beliefs about the likelihood of future events.

1. True

2. False

15. In negotiations involving many issues, you can create a great deal of value by bringing other interested parties to the negotiation table.

1. True

2. False

16. Negotiators understand the importance of reaching a win-win solution: when both sides are satisfied, better partnerships are the result.

1. True

2. False

17. In negotiations, include a "matching right" in your contract; a guarantee that both parties will receive an identical service for an identical price.

1. True

2. False

18. When formulating the initial contract, you can (and should) specify what will happen if one side violates the contract.

1. True

2. False

Knowledge Assessment Questions
ANSWER KEY

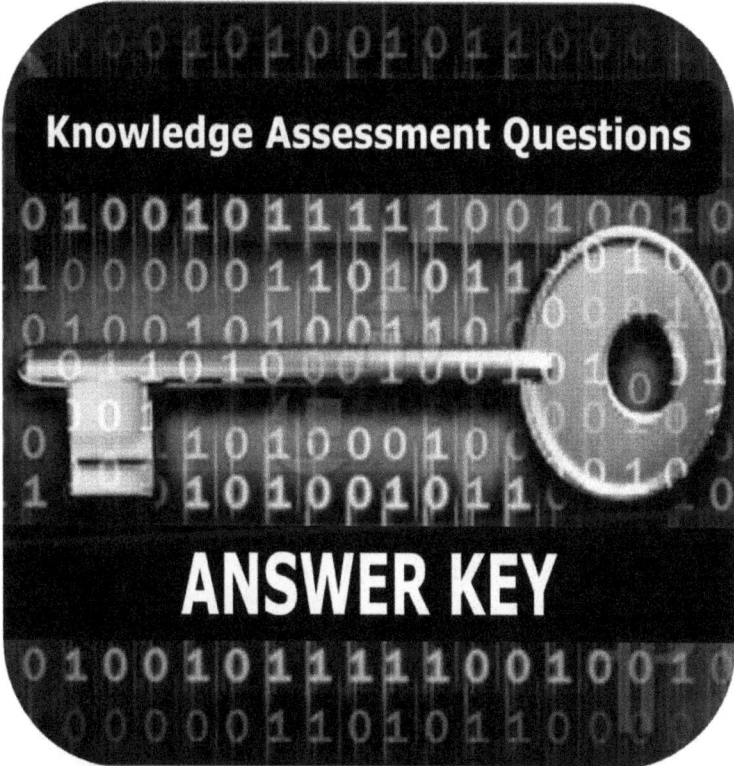

Knowledge Assessment Questions

ANSWER KEY

Domain 01: Knowledge Assessment Answer Key

1. *"A set of policies, tools, and procedures to enable the recovery and continuation of mission-critical technology infrastructure and systems following a natural or human-induced disaster."*

C. Disaster Recovery

The definition listed in this question is the definition of Disaster Recovery.

2. _____ is a set of policies, tools, and procedures to enable the recovery and continuation of mission-critical technology infrastructure and systems following a natural or human-induced disaster.

C. Disaster Recovery

The description listed in this question is the definition of Disaster Recovery.

3. *"Any user- or system-generated action or occurrence that can be identified by a program and has significance for system hardware or software."*

A. Event

The definition listed in this question is the definition of an event. All incidents are events, but not all events are incidents.

4. The three pillars of Business Continuity Planning (BCP) and Disaster Recovery Planning (DRP) are certification and compliance, risk management and audit, and _____.

D. Operational Process Alignment

The three pillars of BCP / DRP are certification and compliance, risk management and audit, and operational process alignment.

5. *"The absolute maximum time that systems can be unavailable without serious and/or negative impact to the organization."*

C. Maximum Allowable Downtime (MAD)

The definition listed in this question is the definition of Maximum Allowable Downtime (MAD).

6. A(n) _____ is a detailed document, maintained and managed by BCP leadership, written to meet a set of specific workflow needs.

B. Work Area Continuity Plan

The description listed in this question is the definition of Work Area Continuity Plan.

7. *"The maximum acceptable amount of data loss, measured in time, that can be incurred without serious and/or negative impact to the organization."*

B. Recovery Point Objective (RPO)

The definition listed in this question is the definition of Recovery Point Objective (RPO).

8. A(n) _____ is a detailed document, maintained and managed by IT leadership, written to meet a set of specific technology needs.

A. Technical Continuity Plan

The description listed in this question is the definition of Technical Continuity Plan.

9. *"The examination and evaluation of non-measurable data using subjective judgement and non-quantifiable methods."*

B. Qualitative Analysis

The definition listed in this question is the definition of qualitative analysis.

10. A(n) _____ is a detailed document written to meet a set of specific response and mitigation needs during an adverse situation.

D. Crisis Management Plan

The description listed in this question is the definition of Crisis Management Plan.

11. Which choice below represents a challenge to the activation of a Business Continuity Plan (BCP)?

E. All of the Above

All of the available choices given pose real-world challenges to the activation of a BCP.

12. A(n) _____ is a consolidated, high-level document written to meet a set of specific business and operational needs.

C. Administrative Continuity Plan

The description listed in this question is the definition of Administrative Continuity Plan.

13. Information Security is a critical business objective in and of itself, and Information Security drives all business objectives.

2. False

Information Security is not a business objective in and of itself, but Information Security underlies all business objectives.

14. Corporate culture can create "shadow policies" that serve to diminish or even negate established formal, written policies.

1. True

15. The Digital Forensics Plan is a general document written to meet a set of specific planning needs when converting data to digital media.

2. False

The Digital Forensics Plan is a detailed document written to meet a set of specific remediation needs during an adverse situation.

16. The Incident Response Plan is a detailed document written to identify and characterize serious events possessing the capability of negatively impacting business operations.

1. True

17. The Business Continuity Plan (BCP) is a monolithic and linear document. It is supported bottom-up, created top-down, and changes every five years.

2. False

The Business Continuity Plan (BCP) is not a monolithic or linear document. It is supported top-down, created bottom-up, and always evolving.

18. The first draft of a policy is rarely adequate, and the maturity level of policies tend to be incremental by nature.

1. True

Domain 02: Knowledge Assessment Answer Key

1. Which choice below does not represent a direct or indirect benefit of conducting a Business Impact Analysis (BIA)?
E. None of the Above

Each choice presented in this question represents a direct or indirect benefit of conducting a BIA.

2. A BIA provides many benefits to the organization, many of which are valuable beyond the scope of a business continuity project and allow the BCP Manager to identify _____.
E. All of the Above

Each choice presented in this question provides benefits to the organization beyond the scope of the BCP.

3. When conducting a Business Impact Analysis (BIA), which choice below would not be considered an intangible cost?
C. Products Cannot be Shipped

Products that cannot be shipped have a monetary value which can be easily calculated, making it a tangible cost.

4. When writing the BIA, _____ would be an example of a tangible financial loss due to a negative impact on a critical business function.
D. Penalties Imposed by Customers

Penalties imposed by customers due to breach of contract have a monetary value which can be easily calculated, making this choice a tangible cost.

5. Which choice below does not represent a component or characteristic of the Business Impact Analysis (BIA) questionnaire process?
D. Review Responses for Conformity

When BCP Managers review BIA questionnaires returned from various units they do so for clarity, not conformity.

6. When writing the BIA, _____ would be an example of an intangible financial loss due to a negative impact on a critical business function.
C. Employee Resignations and Turnover

No BIA can state with absolute certainty the number of employee resignations during a disaster, making it an intangible cost.

7. Which choice below does not represent a component or characteristic of a formal assumption / exception workflow process?
E. All of the Above

The requested is submitted for a functional review, there is no financial review, the assumption must align with the BCP, and all exception approvals must for formally documented and signed.

8. When selecting a BIA Project Manager, _____ is one of the most important attributes the potential candidate must possess to be successful.
A. Comfortable Moderating Discussions

One of the most important attributes of a BIA Project Manager is the ability to be comfortable moderating discussions.

9. Which choice below does not represent a characteristic of selecting questionnaire recipients during a Business Impact Analysis (BIA)?
B. Senior Leadership Identifies Vital Functions

When selecting recipients for BIA questionnaires it will be unit managers, not senior leadership, who will have the subject matter expertise to provide the necessary information.

10. _____ is a topic that is often overlooked by BCP Managers who do not consider "human costs" when creating BIA questionnaires.

B. Employee Morale

BCP Managers need to be aware of the nature of employee morale as it relates to possible resignation and turnover during and after a disaster.

11. Which choice below does not represent a characteristic of potential delayed costs when conducting a Business Impact Analysis (BIA)?

D. Decreased Revenue from Lost Sales

The cost of decreased revenue from lost sales can be measured immediately, making it an incorrect choice as a delayed cost.

12. When a presenter uses slides during a formal presentation, he or she should _____ to ensure the highest probability of a successful outcome.

C. Limit Bullet Points and Text

Limiting bullet points and text in presentation slides is considered to be a "best practice" for formal presentations and training.

13. A Business Inventory Analysis (BIA) provides many benefits to the organization, many of which are valuable beyond the scope of a strategic business plan.

2. False

A Business Impact Analysis (BIA) provides many benefits to the organization, many of which are valuable beyond the scope of a business continuity project.

14. Intangible costs due to the loss of a vital business function can be more difficult to identify but are no less damaging.

1. True

15. A well-run Business Impact Analysis (BIA) will generate good press for the overall disaster recovery planning project from the business' public customer base.

2. False

A well-run Business Impact Analysis (BIA) will build credibility for the overall disaster recovery planning project; a poorly-run BIA will be a disaster unto itself.

16. Once the Business Impact Analysis (BIA) questionnaires have been developed and tested in a single unit, distribute them to all appropriate business units.

1. True

17. Check salary data and key job skills for all selected respondents to help ensure timely completion of the Business Impact Analysis (BIA) questionnaire.

2. False

18. When using the Business Impact Analysis (BIA) questionnaire ensure you ask the right people the right questions; there are many intangible costs with tangible consequences.

1. True

Domain 03: Knowledge Assessment Answer Key

1. Which choice below does not represent a characteristic of the threat landscape posed by the "Internet of Things" (IoT)?
E. None of the Above

All of the choices offered for this question are characteristics of the IoT threat landscape.

2. _____ is a well-established and widely used risk management framework that is best suited for small projects and one-time assessments.
D. OCTAVE Allegro

The description provided in this question is the definition of the OCTAVE Allegro Risk Management Framework.

3. *"The process of identifying and analyzing potential issues that could negatively impact key business initiatives or critical projects in order to help organizations avoid or mitigate those risks."*
C. Risk Analysis

The definition provided in this question is the definition of Risk Analysis.

4. _____ is a well-established and widely used risk management framework with a style that is easily adaptable to other analysis methods.
C. FRAAP

The description provided in this question is the definition of the FRAAP Risk Management Framework.

5. Which choice below does not represent a primary goal or objective when implementing the risk management process?
D. Operate Within Financial Constraints

While financial constraints are always a consideration, they are not a primary consideration of the risk management process.

6. _____ is a well-established and widely used risk management framework that is a detailed quantitative and probabilistic analysis method.

B. FAIR

The description provided in this question is the definition of the FAIR Risk Management Framework.

7. Which choice below represents a characteristic or component of conducting a successful asset inventory in support of a Business Continuity Plan (BCP)?

E. All of the Above

All of the choices offered for this question are characteristics of conducting a successful asset inventory.

8. _____ is a well-established and widely used risk management framework consisting of six steps and replaces the "Certification and Accreditation" model.

A. NIST RMF

The description provided in this question is the definition of the NIST Risk Management Framework.

9. Which choice below does not represent a basic consideration when conducting an asset valuation in support of a Business Continuity Plan (BCP)?

B. Employee Skill Sets

Although employee skills are important, an asset valuation for a BCP focuses on critical systems and functionality/

10. When attempting to identify manufactured risks such as _____, the BCP Manager must emphasize the need to be aware of them even if they cannot be controlled.

D. Underground Gas Pipelines

Underground gas pipelines pose a significant risk to organizations but cannot be controlled by the BCP Manager. All remaining choices presented in this question present mitigable risks.

11. Which choice below does not represent a component, characteristic, or objective of conducting a vulnerability assessment?

D. Based on Capability, Likelihood, Impact

A risk assessment, not a vulnerability assessment, addresses the elements of capability, likelihood, and impact.

12. The six steps associated with the NIST Risk Management Framework are Categorize, Select, Implement, _____, Authorize, and Monitor.

C. Assess

The six steps associated with the NIST Risk Management Framework are Categorize, Select, Implement, Assess, Authorize, and Monitor.

13. Not all third-party service providers can be audited, but for those that can the audit requirement should be considered after the Service Level Agreement (SLA) is renewed.

2. False

Not all third-party service providers can be audited, but for those that can the audit requirement should be negotiated into the Service Level Agreement (SLA).

14. When identifying and predicting the costs of manufactured risks, document the fact the risks exist even if they cannot be controlled or mitigated.

1. True

15. A vulnerability assessment is a useful tool to ensure risk evaluation and mitigation align with business and organizational needs.

2. False

A vulnerability assessment is a useful tool to identify weaknesses visible to threat sources.

16. Creating an Asset Resource Profile provides confidential information for risk mitigation; document the resource profile on an asset inventory page.

1. True

17. Asset inventories are optional information for the Administrative Business Continuity Plan (BCP) that is typically kept in both the BCP and a back-up storage location.

2. False

Asset inventories are critical information for the Technical Business Continuity Plan (BCP) that is typically kept in both the BCP and the asset location.

18. Adapt and utilize established Risk Management reference models based on organizational culture and specific needs.

1. True

Domain 04: Knowledge Assessment Answer Key

1. Which choice below does **not** represent the general characteristics and/or components of a qualitative analysis?
A. Objective and Accurate Analysis

Although a necessary component of risk analysis, qualitative analysis is subjective and prone to error.

2. _____ can be defined as the expected monetary loss that can be expected for an asset due to a risk over a one-year period
D. Annualized Loss Expectancy

The description provided in this question is the definition of Annualized Loss Expectancy.

3. Which choice below does **not** represent a consideration or objective when attempting to determine the severity of impact on data availability?
D. Degrees of Unauthorized Access

Degrees of unauthorized access are considered when determining the severity of impact on data integrity.

4. _____ can be defined as the probability that a risk will occur in a particular year.
A. Annualized Rate of Occurrence

The description provided in this question is the definition of Annualized Rate of Occurrence.

5. Which choice below does **not** represent a consideration or question to be asked when attempting to determine the severity of a specific vulnerability?
C. How Attractive is the Target?

The attractiveness of a target speaks to the issue of risk, not the issue of vulnerability.

6. _____ can be defined as the monetary value expected from the occurrence of a risk on an asset.

B. Single Loss Expectancy

The description provided in this question is the definition of Single Loss Expectancy.

7. Which choice below does **not** represent a challenge to be overcome when attempting to conduct a quantitative analysis?

A. Data Standardized for all Industries

A significant challenge of collecting data for a quantitative analysis is it tends to be industry-specific and skewed.

8. _____ can be defined as the process of determining the fair market or present value of assets.

C. Asset Valuation

The description provided in this question is the definition of Asset Valuation.

9. Which choice below represents a consideration or question to be asked when attempting to determine the actual value of an asset?

E. All of the Above

All choices presented in this question are determinations when determining the actual value of an asset.

10. Most _____ analysis approaches use a relative scale to rate risk exposures based on a set of predefined criteria for each level.

D. Qualitative

Domain 04: *Qualitative and Quantitative Analysis Strategies*

Qualitative analysis uses a relative scale to rate risk exposures based on a set of predefined criteria for each level.

11. Which choice below represents the general characteristics and/or components which exist when defining levels of severity?
E. All of the Above

All choices presented in this question are characteristics which exist when defining levels of severity.

12. A BCP Manager concerned with _____ will focus primarily on unauthorized or unintended access to create, read, update, or delete data ("CRUD").
C. Integrity Severity

Integrity severity will focus primarily on unauthorized or unintended access to create, read, update, or delete data.

13. Most qualitative analysis approaches use a relative scale to rate risk exposures based on a set of predefined criteria for each level.
1. True

14. Developing qualitative risk scales are a great opportunity to design a security focus directly into the risk model.
2. False

Developing qualitative risk scales are a great opportunity to design a business focus directly into the risk model.

15. If you are having trouble qualifying the severity of a vulnerability, many useful questions can be asked to improve clarity.
1. True

16. Many quantitative analysis models have been proposed over the years with complex equations for calculating vulnerabilities.

2. False

Many quantitative analysis models have been proposed over the years with complex equations for calculating risk.

17. Annualized Rate of Occurrence (ARO): calculate probability over time by dividing one year by the predicted likelihood of the event in question.

1. True

18. Integrity severity concerns will focus primarily on unauthorized or unintended access to falsify, steal, or embezzle data.

2. False

Integrity severity concerns will focus primarily on unauthorized or unintended access to create, modify, or delete data ("CRUD").

Domain 05: Knowledge Assessment Answer Key

1. Which choice below does **not** represent the characteristics or objectives of documenting a testing strategy for the Business Continuity Plan (BCP)?

B. Improvisational Testing Creates Compliance

Improvisational testing creates opportunities to test the BCP but cannot be predicted and documented as a testing strategy.

2. The objective of a _____ is to create and work through a BCP that is standardized and understood by all participants.

C. Checklist Test

The description offered in this choice is the definition of a Checklist Test.

3. Which choice below represents a characteristic that must be considered when creating strategies to test Recovery Time Objectives (RTOs)?

C. All Participants Understand Roles

When creating strategies to test Recovery Time Objectives it is critical that all participants understand their roles.

4. The objective of a _____ is to train specific team members, identify omissions, and raise general awareness of the BCP.

D. Table-Top Test

The description offered in this choice is the definition of a Table-Top Test.

5. Which choice below does **not** represent a primary benefit to be considered when testing the Business Continuity Plan (BCP)?

A. Testing Deficiencies Increase BCP Budget

Increasing budgets are a function of management and not an objective of an effective BCP testing strategy.

6. The objective of a _____ is to test the BCP with actual systems without the risk of interrupting the business operation.
B. Parallel Test

The description offered in this choice is the definition of a Parallel Test.

7. Which choice below does **not** represent a characteristic or objective that must be considered when conducting Business Continuity Plan (BCP) Table-Top Testing exercises?
C. Typically a Two-Day Exercise

A Table-Top Test is typically a half-day exercise designed to train specific groups of people and raise awareness.

8. The objective of a _____ is to create a full interruption of the business system to definitively test the BCP.
A. Fail-Over Test

The description offered in this choice is the definition of a Fail-Over Test.

9. Which choice below does **not** represent a potentially suitable event to consider when planning Business Continuity Plan (BCP) improvisational testing exercises?
D. Minor Structural Floods or Fires

Minor structural floods and fires are serious incidents that may test a BCP but can hardly be considered improvisational.

10. _____ can create unique opportunities to execute BCP testing scenarios that are relevant to the business operation.
C. Planned Events

Planned events such as scheduled power outages and facility construction are good opportunities for improvisational tests.

11. Which choice below does **not** represent an appropriate action to consider when debriefing Business Continuity Plan (BCP) testing and exercise participants?

B. Document and Reject Dissenting Opinions

When debriefing BCP testing participants all opinions should be documented but never rejected because they are dissenting.

12. As with all things in the Business Continuity Program, begin setting goals for the testing plan by referring to the _____.

C. Business Impact Analysis

The core of the BCP / DRP is the Business Impact Analysis and encompasses all BCP plans and objectives.

13. To maximize the benefit to the security department while minimizing management involvement, develop a written testing strategy for the Business Continuity Plan (BCP).

2. False

To maximize the benefit to the organization while minimizing costs, develop a written testing strategy for the Business Continuity Plan (BCP).

14. Business Continuity Plan (BCP) testing can be structured to focus on a plans' strengths and gloss over weaknesses; third-party certification addresses this issue.

1. True

15. The best Business Continuity Plan (BCP) testing results come from a clear explanation of the feedback of senior leadership, and training to show them what to do.

2. False

Domain 05: *Implementing the 5 Levels of BCP Testing*

The best Business Continuity Plan (BCP) testing results come from a clear explanation of the responsibilities of team members, and training to show them what to do.

16. Whenever an incident occurs that is covered by the Business Continuity Plan (BCP), conduct an after-action review on the next workday after the recovery.

1. True

17. The objective of Checklist Testing is to create and work through a Business Continuity Plan (BCP) that is unit-specific and understood by senior leadership.

2. False

The objective of Checklist Testing is to create and work through a Business Continuity Plan (BCP) that is standardized and understood by all participants.

18. The objective of a Fail-Over Test is to create a full interruption of the business system to definitively test the Business Continuity Plan (BCP).

1. True

Domain 06: Knowledge Assessment Answer Key

1. Which choice below does **not** represent the characteristics of a poorly planned response to a disaster without the use of a Business Continuity Plan (BCP)?
B. Action Directed by Single Person

A poorly planned response to a disaster will typically lack any type of definitive leadership from a single individual.

2. When an Emergency Operations Center is activated two primary teams are deployed: the _____ Team and the Recovery Team.
B. Containment

When an EOC is activated, there are typically two types of teams deployed: a Containment Team and a Recovery Team.

3. Which choice below represents the characteristics and considerations for a temporary Emergency Operations Center (EOC)?
E. All of the Above

All choices presented in this question represent characteristics of a temporary EOC.

4. An important command function an EOC will undertake will be to _____ when first activated to take control of the decision-making process.
D. Gather Damage Assessments

Gathering damage assessments is a command function of the EOC; all other choices listed are control functions.

5. Which choice below does **not** represent a condition to be considered when discussing the characteristics of an Emergency Operations Center (EOC)?
A. Easily Accessible by Airport

One of the primary considerations when choosing the location for an EOC is that it be easily accessible by road.

6. An important control function an EOC will undertake will be to _____ when first activated to take control of the decision-making process.

C. Control the Flow of Information

Controlling the flow of information is a control function of the EOC; all other choices listed are command functions.

7. Which choice below does **not** represent an item or action to be considered when planning the Uninterruptible Power Supply (UPS) needs of an Emergency Operations Center (EOC)?

C. Use Generator to Recharge UPS

Using a generator to recharge a UPS will divert power away from critical resources relying on the generators' power supply.

8. Prior to _____ electrical support units such as generators and UPS, you must know what they will need to support in the EOC.

E. All of the Above

All of the choices provided for this question must be postponed until the power needs of the EOC have been considered.

9. Which choice below does **not** represent a team member to be considered when planning for the key personnel needs of an Emergency Operations Center (EOC)?

D. Payroll / Finance Manager

The Payroll / Finance Manager serves a critical function on a daily basis but is not a command or control function of the EOC.

10. Most organizations _____ an existing facility with specific capabilities into an Emergency Operations Center as needed.

A. Convert

Most organizations convert an existing facility into an EOC to save money and maximize the utility of their assets.

11. Which choice below does **not** represent a benefit or characteristic to be considered when planning for the use of a Mobile Emergency Operations Center (MEOC)?

C. Does not Require Cellular for Voice / Data

MEOC's require cellular capability for voice and data operations and must be considered during the planning phases.

12. A disaster is not the time to determine what you need in an Emergency Operations Center; _____ will help ensure a faster recovery.

D. Careful Planning

Careful planning will help ensure an organization reduces chaos and recovers more quickly after a disaster.

13. An Emergency Operations Center (EOC) allows organizational management to reassign leadership, locate resources, and focus on daily business operations.

2. False

An Emergency Operations Center (EOC) allows organizational management to reestablish leadership, allocate resources, and focus on containment and recovery.

14. The Emergency Operations Center (EOC) control function involves obtaining and dispatching resources based on the direction of the EOC manager.

1. True

15. When an Emergency Operations Center (EOC) is activated, there are two primary teams: the Management Team and the Support Team.

2. False

When an Emergency Operations Center (EOC) is activated, there are two primary teams: The Containment Team and the Recovery Team.

16. An important staffing consideration is for every member of the Emergency Operations Center (EOC) to have a predesignated and cross-trained backup when possible.

1. True

17. A disaster is the perfect time to determine what you need in an Emergency Operations Center (EOC); observed needs will help ensure faster recovery.

2. False

A disaster is not the time to determine what you need in an Emergency Operations Center (EOC); careful planning will help ensure faster recovery.

18. The Command Center will communicate with teams, news media, vendors, customers, the community, and a broad range of stakeholders.

1. True

Domain 07: Knowledge Assessment Answer Key

1. "*A business location that is used for backup in the event of a disruptive operational disaster at the normal business site and typically does not have the necessary equipment to resume prompt operations.*"

C. Cold Site

The definition provide in this question is the definition for a Disaster Recovery Cold Site.

2. The _____ represents the senior leadership and must be able to manage technical and non-technical activities.

C. Recovery Site Manager

The Recovery Site Manager is the most senior individual at the recovery site and represents the authority of leadership.

3. "*A business location that is used for backup in the event of a disruptive operational disaster at the normal business site and is typically a fully-operational commercial disaster recovery service that allows continuity of operations in a very short period.*"

A. Hot Site

The definition provide in this question is the definition for a Disaster Recovery Hot Site.

4. When a recovery site is activated following a disaster there is no time to argue about job boundaries or _____.

D. Authority

When a recovery site is activated the no one has more authority than the Recovery Site Manager.

5. Which choice below does **not** represent an appropriate consideration when discussing potential locations for a personnel assembly point?

C. Secure and Confidential Location

The location of the recovery site must be well-known and easy to find for every team member expected to participate.

6. The recovery site activity log is used to record significant events during the recovery and helps with post-recovery analysis and _____.

B. Planning

The recovery site activity log will document successes, obstacles, and help the BCP Manager to better plan for future disasters.

7. Which choice below does **not** represent a responsibility of the Recovery Site Manager when assigning tasks to staff?

D. Assign Disaster Site Responsibilities

The Recovery Site Manager has full responsibility of the recovery site; the disaster site will be managed by another team.

8. Validating successful recoveries provides a(n) _____ testing strategy that is useful for catching errors and reducing the need to troubleshoot.

A. Layered

The system for validating successful recoveries is a layered strategy designed to reduce redundant and failed efforts.

9. Which choice below does **not** represent the purpose of a Recovery Activity Log located at a disaster recovery site?

A. Efficient Substitute for Gantt Chart

The data input into the Recovery Site Activity Log will be used to populate the Gannt Chart, not replace it.

10. Designing the recovery site layout is a team effort that requires _____ to be involved in the process.

D. Critical Departments

Critical departments must be a part of the recovery site planning team as they may have critical needs unknown to others.

11. Which choice below does **not** represent a consideration when planning for the use of magnetic back-up media to be transported to the recovery site?

E. None of the Above

All of the choices presented for this question represent planning considerations when transporting magnetic media.

12. The _____ method for team member notification is prone to error and an inefficient option at larger scales.

C. Call Tree

Call trees are a dated method for performing communication and tend to be inefficient and prone to error.

13. A conditioned response is critical to effective crisis management; time for recovery is decreased when teams can be tasked quickly.

1. True

14. Different levels of management and team members with different roles will need to hear the same broadcast messages to ensure everyone is informed.

2. False

Different levels of management and team members with different roles will not need to hear the same broadcast messages.

15. When a recovery site is activated following a disaster, there is no time to argue about job boundaries or authority.

1. True

16. The "call tree" method for team member notification is prone to error and only an efficient option for larger organizations.

2. False

The "call tree" method for team member notification is prone to error and an inefficient option at larger scales.

17. The recovery site activity log is used to record significant events during the recovery and helps with post-recovery analysis and planning.

1. True

18. Duplication of data provides an efficient compression, single instance storage solution that reduces required storage space and recovery time.

2. False

Deduplication of data provides an efficient compression, single instance storage solution that reduces required storage space and recovery time.

Domain 08: Knowledge Assessment Answer Key

1. Which choice below does **not** qualify as a phase of a pandemic as defined by the World Health Organization (WHO)?
B. Human to Animal (Limited)

Human to animal contact does not qualify as a phase of a pandemic as defined by the World Health Organization (WHO)?

2. Seasonal influenza has the distinctive characteristic of _____ that distinguishes it from pandemic influenza counterpart.
D. Some Immunity Exists

Unlike pandemic influenza a degree of immunity to the seasonal influenza virus exists within the affected populations.

3. Which choice below does **not** represent a valid consideration for Senior Leadership when planning for post-epidemic or post-pandemic actions and operations?
E. All of the Above

All of the choices presented for this question represent post-epidemic and post-pandemic considerations for management.

4. Pandemic influenza has the distinctive characteristic of _____ that distinguishes it from epidemic influence counterpart.
C. Unpredictable Patterns

Unlike epidemic influenza which typically occurs seasonally a pandemic influenza has no predictable pattern.

5. Which choice below does **not** represent a valid fact or statistic regarding influenza epidemics?
C. Infection Radius: Up to 12 Feet

According to documented statistics a person with influenza has an infection radius of six feet.

6. Epidemics and Pandemics require unique solutions and unique BCP teams that should include members with _____.
B. Medical Experience

BCP teams should make every effort secure team members with medical experience due to nature of this potential threat.

7. Which choice below does **not** represent a valid consideration for Human Resource Management when planning for influenza epidemics or pandemics?
B. Mandatory Immunization Policy

Although influenza vaccinations provide degrees of protection no person can be compelled against their will to get one.

8. The Epidemic / Pandemic BCP is based on a(n) _____ Business Impact Analysis and will vary based on unit responsibility.
A. Fluctuating

Influenza requires a BCP based on a fluctuating BIA due to the responsibilities and locations of individuals and business units.

9. Which choice below does **not** represent a valid fact or statistic regarding vulnerable populations impacted by influenza epidemics?
D. People with Body Mass Index ≥ 20

People with a Body Mass Index that is ≥ 40 are considered to be unhealthy and a vulnerable population to influenza.

10. Human Resources and IT are the core of the Epidemic / Pandemic BCP and can identify _____ impacted by risk mitigation efforts.
D. Company Policies

Human Resources and IT can adjust attendance and remote worker policies to better mitigate the influenza threat.

11. Which choice below does **not** represent a valid concern when conducting an Epidemic / Pandemic Risk Assessment?

C. Cost of International Travel

When conducting an Epidemic / Pandemic Risk Assessment international travel itself, not its cost, is a concern.

12. The _____ phase of a Pandemic as defined by the WHO is typically the phase at which an Epidemic / Pandemic BCP is initiated.

C. Country to Country (region)

The spread of influenza at a county to country (regional) level is typically when an Epidemic / Pandemic BCP is initiated.

13. The World Health Organization has divided pandemics into seven phases; the last phase will dictate when a disaster is declared.

2. False

The World Health Organization has divided pandemics into six phases; the phase will dictate when a disaster is declared.

14. Maintain vigilance as epidemic / pandemic cases decline and utilize continuous communication until the event is officially declared over.

1. True

15. When writing a Pandemic Plan into the Business Continuity Plan (BCP), it is important to consider the personal possessions of organizational staff.

2. False

Domain 08: *Preparing for Epidemics and Pandemics*

When writing a Pandemic Plan into the Business Continuity Plan (BCP), it is important to consider the family members of organizational staff.

16. Human Resources and IT are the core of the Epidemic / Pandemic Business Continuity Plan (BCP) and can identify company policies impacted by risk mitigation efforts.
1. True

17. The Epidemic / Pandemic Risk Assessment is based on a predicted Business Impact Analysis (BIA) and will vary based on those writing the assessment.
2. False

The Epidemic / Pandemic Risk Assessment is based on a fluctuating Business Impact Analysis (BIA) and will vary based on unit responsibility.

18. Despite the distinction of definitions between epidemics and pandemics, an epidemic is simply a localized pandemic.
1. True

Domain 09: Knowledge Assessment Answer Key

1. Which choice below does **not** qualify as one of the five established characteristics of cloud computing?

C. Incremental Rigidity

Rapid elasticity is one of the five established characteristics of cloud computing and one of its most powerful selling points.

2. Hybrid clouds contain elements of public, private, and community cloud models to varying degrees based on _____.

A. Customer Needs

Hybrid clouds contain elements of public, private, and community cloud models to varying degrees based on customer needs.

3. Which choice below accurately describes the services offered to customers using Hybrid Cloud solutions?

E. All of the Above

All of the choices provided to the question above accurately describe hybrid cloud services offered to customers.

4. Community clouds provide infrastructure and _____ that is owned and operated by affinity groups and similar organizations.

B. Functionality

Affinity groups and organizations with similar functionality requirements may find community cloud a viable solution.

5. Which choice below does **not** qualify as one of the actions taken when determining an organizations' existing operational state?

D. Interview Cloud Providers

Determining an organizations' existing operational state is an internal process that does not need cloud provider input.

6. In the PaaS model, the cloud service provider offers not only the IaaS capability but provides the customer with _____ as well.

C. Operating Systems

Cloud providers provide customers utilizing the PaaS model a wide variety of operating systems based on their needs.

7. Which choice below does **not** accurately describe the services offered to customers by Private Cloud Providers?

C. Segments Owned by Organizations

When segments of the cloud infrastructure and functionality are owned by organizations it is a community cloud environment.

8. Managing data and its required infrastructure is neither a core function of most organizations nor is it a _____ to the business process.

A. Profit Center

Managing data and its required infrastructure is not a core function or a profit center to the business process.

9. Which choice below does **not** qualify as a valid reason for an organization to consider migrating from a legacy system to a cloud solution?

A. Service Costs not Included in Cloud Contract

One of the reasons businesses consider migrating to the cloud is because service costs are included in provider contracts.

10. Cloud services are typically offered in _____ models based on provider capability and customer needs.

D. Three

Cloud services are typically offered in three models to the majority of customers: IaaS, PaaS, and SaaS.

11. Which choice below does **not** reflect the characteristics that cloud customers will experience using the Software as a Service (SaaS) model?

C. Customer Provides Operating System

All customer using the SaaS model will have the benefits of the PaaS model as well which includes operating systems.

12. Despite many functions and configurations, _____ is one of the five characteristics officially accepted as part of the cloud computing definition.

B. Measured Service

Measured (metered) service is one of the cloud characteristics and an attractive "pay as needed" solution.

13. Despite many functions and configurations, NIST lists ten characteristics that are accepted as part of the cloud computing definition.

2. False

Despite many functions and configurations, NIST lists five characteristics that are accepted as part of the cloud computing definition.

14. Hybrid clouds contain elements of public, private, and community cloud models to varying degrees based on customer needs.

1. True

15. Organizations tend to underutilize a technical resource (potential failure) or overutilize a technical resource (wasted money).

2. False

Organizations tend to underutilize a technical resource (wasted money) or overutilize a technical resource (potential failure).

16. Private clouds are owned and operated by individual organizations for the specific use of their staff, customers, and vendors.

1. True

17. Unless organizations use a cloud environment, they cannot transfer the risk or liability associated with disclosure of Personally Identifiable Information (PII).

2. False

Even in a cloud environment, organizations cannot transfer the risk or liability associated with disclosure of Personally Identifiable Information.

18. In the Software as a Service (SaaS) model, the customer receives all the underlying IaaS and PaaS capabilities, as well as end user applications.

1. True

Domain 10: Knowledge Assessment Answer Key

1. There are six defined phases in the Cloud Data Life Cycle. What phase immediately follows the "store" phase?
B. Use

The six phases of the Cloud Data Life Cycle in order are create, store, use, share, archive, and delete.

2. Despite many functions and configurations, _____ is one of the five characteristics officially accepted as part of the cloud computing definition.
B. Measured Service

Measured service is one of the five characteristics officially accepted as part of the cloud computing definition.

3. Which option below does **not** accurately reflect a characteristic or action associated with the "Create Data" phase in the Cloud Development Life Cycle?
C. Use a Cryptosystem with a Low Work Factor

Using a cryptosystem with a high work factor provides the level of performance needed when creating data in the cloud.

4. When considering cloud architecture, _____ is one of the key characteristics of the volume storage model.
A. Higher Flexibility and Performance

The volume storage model has higher flexibility and performance than other storage models in cloud computing.

5. Which option below does **not** accurately reflect a benefit or characteristic of "Egress Monitoring" when considering the implementation of a Data Loss Prevention solution?
A. Data Assimilation Control Mechanism

An egress monitoring solution does not assimilate data but analyzes it prior to leaving a predefined network boundary.

6. When considering cloud architecture, _____ is one of the key characteristics of the object-based storage model.

C. Centralized Data Management

Centralized data management is a feature of the object-based storage model in cloud computing.

7. Which option below presents the least attractive Cloud Data Security option when considering the topic of Obfuscation, Masking and Anonymization?

B. Shuffling

Although shuffling is an accepted method of obfuscation it poses a risk by using actual production data that can be accessed.

8. A(n) _____ is a form of data caching typically located near geophysical locations of high demand and use.

D. Content Delivery Network

A Content Delivery Network is a form of data caching typically located near geophysical locations of high demand and use.

9. Which option below does **not** accurately reflect a characteristic or action associated with the "Share Data" phase in the Cloud Development Life Cycle?

E. None of the Above

All the choices for this question reflect characteristics associated with the "Share" phase in the Cloud Development Life Cycle.

10. In certain instances customers using cloud provider solutions may find it necessary to _____ data and use a representation of data instead.

B. Obscure

Customers may choose to use obfuscation, masking, and anonymization to obscure data stored in cloud environments.

11. Which option below does **not** accurately reflect a characteristic or action associated with "Volume Storage" when considering the structure of Cloud architecture?

C. Lower Administrative Overhead

Volume storage provides functionality and performance that tends to require a higher degree of administrative overhead.

12. A(n) _____ monitoring solution will examine data leaving the production environment and react based on preestablished rules and parameters.

A. Egress

An egress monitoring solution will examine data leaving a network boundary and react based on rules and parameters.

13. Data stored in the cloud tends to have different needs as data stored in legacy systems and should be treated in a unique and proper manner.

2. False

Data stored in the cloud tends to have the same needs as data stored in legacy systems and should be treated in the same manner.

14. An egress monitoring solution will examine data leaving the production environment and react based on preestablished rules and parameters.

1. True

15. Operations within a legacy environment will require remote access with secured connections (typically a username and password).
2. False

Operations within a cloud environment will require remote access with secured connections (typically an encrypted tunnel).

16. In certain instances customers using cloud provider solutions may find it necessary to obscure data and use a representation of data instead.
1. True

17. Archived data is stored for long periods of time; longer timeframes will tend to reduce the requirement for special security considerations.
2. False

Archived data is stored for long periods of time; longer timeframes will require special security considerations.

18. Like its legacy environment counterpart, cloud computing solutions have a significant dependency on encryption to operate.
1. True

Domain 11: Knowledge Assessment Answer Key

1. Which option below does **not** accurately reflect a characteristic or action associated with Cloud Platform Risks?

B. Provider Owns Civil Liability

The cloud customer owns all civil liabilities associated with cloud platform risks at all times and under all conditions.

2. A _____ configuration is a legacy configuration of a datacenter with distributed computing capabilities.

D. Private Cloud

A private cloud configuration is a legacy configuration of a datacenter with distributed computing capabilities.

3. Which option below does **not** accurately reflect a characteristic or action associated with a Private Cloud when considering data security risks?

D. Reduced Organizational Control

Customers maintain complete organizational control when managing and mitigating risks in the private cloud.

4. A _____ configuration is one in which resources are allocated, shared, and dispersed among affinity groups.

B. Community Cloud

A community cloud configuration is one in which resources are allocated, shared, and dispersed among affinity groups.

5. Which option below does **not** accurately reflect a characteristic or actions associated with the Public Cloud when considering data security risks?

E. None of the Above

All of the choices provided for this question accurately reflect data security risks associated with using public cloud services.

6. A _____ configuration is one in which a company offers cloud services to any entity wanting to become a cloud customer.
C. Public Cloud

A public cloud configuration is one in which a company offers cloud services to any entity wanting to become a cloud customer.

7. Which option below does **not** accurately reflect a characteristic or action associated with data security risks when considering utilizing the Platform as a Service (PaaS) model in a Public Cloud?
C. O/S Administered by Customer

In the PaaS service model the operating system is administered and maintained by the cloud service provider.

8. Many potential threats posed by _____ require attenuation via the use of controls that can only be implemented by the provider.
A. Virtualization

The cloud service provider manages all virtualization and is the only party capable of attenuating potential virtualization threats.

9. Which option below does **not** accurately reflect a characteristic or action associated with data security risks when considering utilizing virtualization capabilities in a Public Cloud?
D. Attackers Prefer Type 1 Hypervisors

Attackers prefer Type II hypervisors due to the larger attack surface created by the existing operating system.

10. Unlike a legacy environment, a customer conducting operations in the cloud will not be able to conduct _____ without the provider.

D. Local Computing

A customer completely reliant on the public cloud for service will not have the resources available for local computing if needed.

11. Which option below does **not** accurately reflect a characteristic or action associated with data security risks when considering utilizing a Private Cloud environment?

E. None of the Above

A private cloud is subject to the same data security risks as those that exist for legacy datacenter environments.

12. _____ can be caused when the provider goes out of business, is acquired by another interest, or ceases operation for any reason.

C. Vendor Lock-Out

Vendor lock-out can be caused when the provider goes out of business or ceases operation for any reason.

13. Because the cloud customer and provider will each process data, they will share responsibilities and risks associated with the data.

1. True

14. Unlike a legacy environment, a customer conducting operations in the cloud will be able to conduct limited local computing without the provider.

2. False

Unlike a legacy environment, a customer conducting operations in the cloud will not be able to conduct local computing without the provider.

15. A private cloud configuration is a legacy configuration of a datacenter with associated distributed computing capabilities.
1. True

16. Although many threats to cloud computing are the same faced in legacy operations, they manifest in the same way and present the same types of risk.
2. False

Although many threats to cloud computing are the same faced in legacy operations, they may manifest in novel ways and present new risks.

17. In a public cloud configuration, a company offers cloud services to any entity wanting to become a cloud customer.
1. True

18. In the Software as a Service (SaaS) model, the customer will only have the Platform as a Service (PaaS) model risks and responsibilities.
2. False

In the Software as a Service (SaaS) model, the customer will have all Platform as a Service (PaaS) and Infrastructure as a Service (IaaS) risks as well.

Domain 12: Knowledge Assessment Answer Key

1. Which option below does **not** accurately reflect a characteristic or goal of the relationship between Cloud Service Providers and Cloud Customers?

C. Customer: Maximize Expenses

Customers tend to use cloud services for benefits such as the ability to maximize capability and to minimize expenses.

2. Some element of _____ exists between the customer and the provider because they have somewhat different goals.

D. Adversarial Relationship

Some element of adversarial relationship exists between the customer and provider because they have different goals.

3. Which option below does **not** accurately reflect a characteristic of the shared responsibility between the Cloud Service Provider and the Cloud Customer for Monitoring and Testing management?

B. Increases Risk of Harm and Disclosure

The shared responsibility of monitoring and testing in a cloud environment decreases the risk of harm and data disclosure.

4. The cloud provider must apply the proper security controls according to a customers' relevant regulatory frameworks and _____.

C. Planned Usage

Regulatory frameworks and the planned usage of services will dictate the security controls provided to the cloud customer.

5. Which option below does **not** accurately reflect a responsibility of the Cloud Service Provider when considering the protection of its physical plant?

E. None of the Above

All the choices offered for this question represent responsibilities of the cloud provider protecting its physical plant.

6. In _____ cloud service models, the customer and their users will need to access and modify the data at various levels.

B. All

In all cloud service models, the customer and their users will need to access and modify the data at various levels.

7. Which option below does **not** accurately reflect a characteristic or challenge for the Cloud Customer when considering the lack of allowed access to a Cloud Provider environment?

D. Decreases Trust in the Cloud Provider

Limited access to the providers' facility increases trust because cloud customers realize all customers are similarly restricted.

8. By reviewing the type of _____ utilized by the cloud customer, the responsibilities can be assigned to the appropriate party.

A. Service Model

The service model chosen by the cloud customer will dictate how responsibilities are assigned to the appropriate party.

9. Which option below does **not** accurately reflect a responsibility of the Cloud Service Provider when considering the protection of its secure logical framework?

B. Non-Attenuation of Potential Risks

The provider is responsible for attenuating potential risks as part of the protection of its logical framework

10. The _____ is a large attack surface and offers many potential vectors to malicious actors if not secured correctly.

D. Operating System

The operating system is a large attack surface and offers many potential vectors to malicious actors if not secured correctly.

11. Which option below does **not** accurately reflect a responsibility of the Cloud Service Provider when considering the protection of its secure networking capability?

D. Ensure Use of "Data Encryption Standard" (DES)

DES is a dated and weak form of encryption that can be easily compromised and has not been advocated since 2002.

12. In addition to securing the hardware components the cloud provider must ensure that the _____ are equally protected.

C. Logical Elements

In addition to securing the hardware components the provider must ensure that the logical elements are equally protected.

13. Some element of adversarial relationship exists between the customer and the cloud provider because they have somewhat different goals.

1. True

14. An area where cloud providers and cloud customers often fail to find common ground in sharing responsibilities is in security monitoring and testing.

2. False

An area where cloud providers and cloud customers may find common ground in sharing responsibilities is in security monitoring and testing.

15. In addition to securing the hardware components, the cloud provider must ensure that the logical framework elements are equally protected.

1. True

16. The cloud provider will have a limited number of reasons to allow the customer any physical access to the facility containing customer data.

2. False

The cloud provider will not have any reason to allow the customer any physical access to the facility containing customer data.

17. The cloud provider must apply the proper security controls according to a customers' relevant regulatory frameworks and planned usage.

1. True

18. The operating system in a cloud environment is a smaller attack surface and offers limited potential vectors to malicious actors if not secured correctly.

2. False

The operating system in a cloud environment is a large attack surface and offers many potential vectors to malicious actors if not secured correctly.

Domain 13: Knowledge Assessment Answer Key

1. Which option below does **not** accurately reflect a characteristic or goal of Criminal Law?

D. Laws Enacted by Federal Agencies

Criminal laws are enacted by state legislatures as opposed to federal agencies.

2. _____ involves all legal matters where the government conflicts with any person, group or entity that violates various statutes.

D. Criminal Law

Any matter in which the government is in conflict with any person or entity falls within the scope of criminal law.

3. Which option below is the most widely accepted standard used for Cloud Computing in an international environment when considering "Forensic Requirement" issues?

D. ISO/IEC 27050:2016 (eDiscovery)

ISO/IEC 27050:2016 is the most widely used standard in cloud computing for "forensic requirement" issues.

4. _____ refers to the process of identifying and obtaining evidence for prosecutorial or litigation purposes.

C. eDiscovery

eDiscovery refers to the process of identifying and obtaining evidence for prosecutorial or litigation purposes.

5. Which option below does **not** accurately reflect a characteristic or goal of Civil Law?

C. Adopted for Private and Public Entities

Civil laws are enacted for the specific purpose of resolving disputes solely between private entities.

6. _____ is the body of laws and statutes that deal with personal or community-based law.
C. Civil Law

Civil law is the body of laws and statutes that deal with personal or community-based law.

7. Which option below does **not** accurately reflect a characteristic or goal of Cloud Computing in an international environment when considering "Chain of Custody" issues?
A. Minimal Gaps in the Control Timeline

The chain of custody mandates that absolutely no gaps in the control timeline exist to maintain the integrity of the evidence.

8. Due to the _____ nature of cloud computing, many geographic disparities may present critical personal and data privacy issues.
D. Decentralized

The decentralized nature of cloud computing creates geographic disparities that may present critical data security issues.

9. Which option below does **not** accurately reflect a characteristic or goal of Administrative Law?
B. Enacted by State Legislatures

Administrative law is not enacted by state legislatures but can be enforced to some degree by state agencies.

10. _____ is a body of law that affects most people; it is not created by legislatures, but by executive decision and function.

B. Administrative Law

Administrative law is a body of law that affects most people; it is created and enforced by executive decision and function.

11. Which option below does **not** accurately reflect a characteristic or goal of Cloud Computing in an international environment when considering "eDiscovery" issues?

B. Not Impacted by Contractual Agreements

Contractual agreements between international cloud computing parties can have a significant impact on "eDiscovery" issues.

12. _____ is a term used to describe the processes associated with determining what legal jurisdiction will hear disputes.

A. Doctrine of the Proper Law

The *Doctrine of Proper Law* describes the processes that determine what legal jurisdiction will hear disputes.

13. Criminal law involves all legal matters where a business entity conflicts with any person, group or entity that violates various statutes.

2. False

Criminal law involves all legal matters where the government conflicts with any person, group or entity that violates various statutes.

14. Decentralized data and its movement, storage, and processing across geographic boundaries leads to complex challenges for forensics.

1. True

15. Administrative law is a body of law that affects most people; it is created by legislatures and enforced by executive decision and function.

2. False

Administrative law is a body of law that affects most people; it is not created by legislatures, but by executive decision and function.

16. Electronic Discovery (eDiscovery) refers to the process of identifying and obtaining evidence for prosecutorial or litigation purposes.

1. True

17. Intercontinental law determines how to settle disputes and manage relationships between countries and their respective entities.

2. False

International law determines how to settle disputes and manage relationships between countries and their respective entities.

18. The Privacy Regulation supersedes the Data Directive and ends the Safe Harbor program, replacing it with a program called Privacy Shield.

1. True

Domain 14: Knowledge Assessment Answer Key

1. Which option below does **not** accurately reflect a characteristic or concern of Cloud Computing when considering data security in diverse geographic locations?
A. Jurisdictions with Similar Governance

Jurisdictions with unique and dissimilar governance pose risks to data security in diverse geographical locations.

2. A great deal of the difficulty in managing the legal aspects of cloud computing stems from the _____ of the cloud assets themselves.
B. Design

Difficulty managing the legal aspects of cloud computing stems from the design of the cloud assets themselves.

3. Which option below does **not** accurately reflect a metric intended to be measured by a Service Level Agreement (SLA)?
A. Financial Metrics

SLAs can measure a wide variety of performance metrics, but financial performance is a function of operational management.

4. The _____ risk management framework is a methodology for handling all risk in a holistic, comprehensive, and continual manner.
C. NIST SP 800-37

The NIST SP 800-37 RMF methodology handles risk in a holistic, comprehensive, and continual manner.

5. Which option below does **not** accurately reflect a characteristic or concern when considering the creation of organizational policies in Cloud environments?
B. Regulation Can Increase Risk Appetite

Organizations creating policies for cloud computing will tend to discover that regulation can decrease risk appetite.

6. _____ are a foundational element of governance and risk management programs and ensure companies operate within their risk profiles.
C. Policies

Policies are a foundational element of governance and ensure companies operate within their risk management profiles.

7. Which option below does **not** accurately reflect a characteristic or function of a Service Contract or its attached Service Level Agreement (SLA)?
D. SLA: Stipulates Penalties

Although SLAs will outline expected performance metrics it is the service contract that will stipulate penalties.

8. While both the service contracts and SLA may contain numerical values, the _____ will expressly include metrics to determine if contractual goals are met.
D. Service Level Agreement

Although SLAs and contracts will both contain numerical values, the SLA includes metrics that determine contractual goals.

9. Which option below does **not** accurately reflect a characteristic or concern when engaging stakeholders as an organization considers a migration to a cloud environment?
C. Existing Policies Cannot be Malleable

Organizations migrating to cloud computing must have malleable policies that can change with business processes.

10. The variety and vagaries of _____ law make the regulatory stakeholders and their input complicated for cloud services.

D. Multijurisdictional

The variety and vagaries of multijurisdictional law make any regulatory input complicated for cloud computing.

11. Which option below does **not** accurately reflect a characteristic or goal of the European Union Agency for Network and Information Security Risk Management Framework?

D. Concerned about Complete / Secure Data Deletion

One of the eight listed security risks identified by ENISA is the deletion of incomplete and/or insecure data.

12. It is vitally important that both the customer and the cloud provider focus on _____ and the challenges of cloud computing.

A. Risk Management

It is vital that cloud customers and providers focus on risk management and the challenges of cloud computing.

13. A great deal of the difficulty in managing the legal aspects of cloud computing stems from the design of the cloud policies and procedures.

2. False

A great deal of the difficulty in managing the legal aspects of cloud computing stems from the design of the cloud assets themselves.

14. It is important that the cloud customer consider all possible situations and risks associated with cloud business processes and requirements when signing Service Level Agreements (SLAs).

1. True

15. Identifying and engaging relevant business models is vital to the success of any cloud computing discussions, programs, or projects.

2. False

Identifying and engaging relevant stakeholders is vital to the success of any cloud computing discussions, programs, or projects.

16. The most important documents establishing, defining, and enforcing the relationship between the customer and provider are contracts and Service Level Agreements (SLAs).

1. True

17. Once a policy has been formally accepted, it must be approved by the Board of Directors and added to the Business Continuity Plan (BCP).

2. False

Once a policy has been formally accepted, it must be published and disseminated among those affected by the policy.

18. The European Union Agency for Network and Information Security (ENISA) is international within Europe, but not globally accepted like ISO.

1. True

Domain 15: Knowledge Assessment Answer Key

1. Which option below does **not** accurately reflect a reason why parties engaged in a business venture would choose to utilize a formal contract?

A. Good Contracts Win Disputes

Parties engaged in a business venture would choose to utilize a formal contract to prevent disputes from happening.

2. When reviewing contracts and service level agreements, consider the use of _____ to help ensure a consistent approach.

D. Checklists

When reviewing contracts and service level agreements, consider the use of checklists to help ensure a consistent approach.

3. Which choice below does **not** accurately reflect a component to be taken under consideration when drafting a general contract review checklist?

E. None of the Above

All the choices listed for this question would reflect components to be considered when drafting a general checklist.

4. IT contract and service level agreement terms can be organized into three groups: Prime Clauses, General Clauses, and _____.

C. Boilerplate Clauses

IT contract and SLA terms can be organized into three groups: Prime Clauses, General Clauses, and Boilerplate Clauses.

5. Which choice below does **not** accurately reflect a reason why choosing the best possible option over "fairness" during contract negotiations is the correct strategy?

D. May Reject Economic Common Sense

A reason why choosing the best possible option over "fairness" is to avoid rejecting economic common sense solutions.

6. Most lawsuits arise from contracts that are not clear, complete, and that do not express the agreement as it was _____ by the parties.

C. Understood

Most lawsuits arise from contracts that are not clear, complete, and are not understood by the parties.

7. Which choice below does **not** accurately reflect the function and purpose of a Boilerplate Clause in a formal legal contract?

B. General and Specific Indemnity

The topics of general and specific indemnity are typically found in the General Clause section of a formal legal contract.

8. Customers should protect themselves against _____ and ensure all promises address the expectation of help needed.

D. Unclear Descriptions

Parties should protect themselves against unclear descriptions and ensure all promises address the expectation of help needed.

9. Which choice below does **not** accurately reflect one of the five standard components of a formal legal contract?

C. Secondary Clauses

The five components are Introduction and Recitals, Descriptions, Prime Clauses, General Clauses, and Boilerplate Clauses.

10. You cannot predict what issues may arise in a business relationship, so you cannot know when _____ will become vital.

B. Boilerplate Clauses

You cannot predict what issues may arise in a business relationship, so Boilerplate Clauses may become vital.

11. Which choice below does **not** accurately reflect the function and purpose of a General Clause in a formal legal contract?

A. Choice of Law and Courts

The topic of choice of law and courts are typically found in the Boilerplate Clause section of a formal legal contract.

12. The one characteristic shared by all elements of _____ is that they generate the most disagreement, debate, and compromise.

A. General Clauses

General Clauses tend to generate the most disagreement, debate and compromise between parties in contract negotiations.

13. The best way to avoid arguments in a business relationship is to write down the parties' expectations ahead of time.

1. True

14. When reviewing contracts and Service Level Agreements, consider the use of committees and teams to help ensure a consistent approach.

2. False

When reviewing contracts and Service Level Agreements, consider the use of checklists to help ensure a consistent approach.

15. Each party has a choice about whether to enter into a contract; neither side owes the other any special considerations or terms.

1. True

16. You cannot predict what issues may arise in a business relationship, so you cannot know when "Boilerplate Clauses" will need to be included in the contract.

2. False

You cannot predict what issues may arise in a business relationship, so you cannot know when "Boilerplate Clauses" will become vital.

17. Customers should protect themselves against unclear descriptions in contracts and ensure all promises address the expectation of help needed.

1. True

18. The one characteristic shared by General Clauses in contracts is that they are the easiest to understand and warrant the least amount of attention.

2. False

The one characteristic shared by General Clauses in contracts is that they generate the most disagreement, debate, and compromise.

Domain 16: Knowledge Assessment Answer Key

1. Which option below is **not** a provision of an enforceable contract?

D. Non-Agreement

For a contract to exist between parties there must be agreement, or there will be no contract to enforce.

2. In negotiation, parties often reach impasse because they have different beliefs about the likelihood of _____.

D. Future Events

In negotiation, parties often reach impasse because they have different beliefs about the likelihood of future events.

3. Which option below does **not** accurately reflect a characteristic of the negotiation strategy of attempting to search for post-settlement settlements?

C. See if Contract Can be Terminated

Post-settlement settlements seek to increase the benefits of the contract for both parties, not terminate the contract itself.

4. Negotiators understand the importance of reaching a(n) _____ solution; when both sides are satisfied, better partnerships are the result.

C. Win-Win

It is important for negotiators to seek win-win solutions so all parties to the contract feel satisfied with the conditions.

5. When a Service Level Agreement (SLA) has a "guaranteed uptime" requirement, which option listed below would not be a reason to explore that requirement in further detail?

C. Downtime Refunds > Actual Losses

An SLA may stipulate financial penalties on a provider for not meeting uptime metrics, but losses may still exceed refunds.

6. In negotiation, include a _____ in your contract; a guarantee that one side can match any offer that the other side later receives.
C. Matching Right

Try to include a matching right in your contract; a guarantee that one side can match any offer that the other side later receives.

7. Which option below does **not** accurately reflect a characteristic of the negotiation strategy of attempting to negotiate damages early in the process?
D. Removes a New Issue in the Negotiation

Discussing penalties for breach of performance early in the negotiation process brings a new bargaining issue to the table.

8. When formulating the _____ contract you can, and should, specify what will happen if one side violates the contract.
D. Initial

When formulating the initial contract you can, and should, specify what will happen if one side violates the contract.

9. Which option below does **not** accurately reflect a reason why parties engaged in a business contract must ensure the Service Level Agreement (SLA) scales with the business over time?
B. Businesses Do Not Change in Size Dramatically

A contract must ensure the SLA can be scaled over time because businesses can unexpectedly change in size dramatically.

10. A(n) _____ cannot violate the law in any manner and can become void if either party acts in an illegal fashion.
B. Contract

A contract cannot violate the law in any manner and can become void if either party acts in an illegal fashion.

11. Which option below does **not** accurately reflect a characteristic of the negotiation strategy of attempting to make a contingency agreement?
A. Talks Postponed During the Disagreement

Contingency agreements made during the negotiation process can keep the talks continuing even if both parties disagree.

12. A conversation should **not** end once a contract has been negotiated as either party to the contract may benefit from a potential _____.
A. Post-Settlement Settlement

Continued conversations after the contract has been negotiated may lead to post-settlement settlements and benefit all parties.

13. A contract cannot violate the state law in which it was written and can become void if both parties to the contract act in an illegal fashion.
2. False

A contract cannot violate any law in any manner and can become void if either party to the contract acts in an illegal fashion.

14. In negotiations, parties often reach an impasse because they have different beliefs about the likelihood of future events.
1. True

15. In negotiations involving many issues, you can create a great deal of value by bringing other interested parties to the negotiation table.

2. False

In negotiations involving many issues, you can create a great deal of value by making multiple equivalent simultaneous offers (MESO).

16. Negotiators understand the importance of reaching a win-win solution: when both sides are satisfied, better partnerships are the result.

1. True

17. In negotiations, include a "matching right" in your contract; a guarantee that both parties will receive an identical service for an identical price.

2. False

In negotiations, include a "matching right" in your contract; a guarantee that one side can match any offer that the other side later receives.

18. When formulating the initial contract, you can (and should) specify what will happen if one side violates the contract.

1. True

C)DRRM Certification Exam Voucher

CERTIFIED

Disaster Response & Recovery Manager

USE THE CODE BELOW TO RECEIVE A

10% Discount

P2A 2022

CERTIFICATION EXAM VOUCHER

For more information regarding the purchase of exam vouchers and scheduling your exam in the Technical College System of Georgia LMS, please contact our office by phone or email.

OFFICE:

912.335.2217

EMAIL:

michael.kaplan@phase2advantage.com

PHASE2

ΛDVΛNTΛGE

The Future of Immersive Cybersecurity Education

www.phase2advantage.com

C)DRRM Certification Exam Voucher

For more information regarding the purchase of exam vouchers and scheduling your exam in the Technical College System of Georgia LMS, please contact our office by phone or email.

OFFICE:
912.335.2217

EMAIL:
michael.kaplan@phase2advantage.com

PHASE2
ΛDVΛNTΛGE
The Future of Immersive Cybersecurity Education

www.phase2advantage.com

www.ingramcontent.com/pod-product-compliance
Lightning Source LLC
Chambersburg PA
CBHW060330220326
41598CB00023B/2659